Introduction

The **Welsh Highland Railway**, running between Caernarfon and Porthmadog, where it connects with the Ffestiniog Railway, is the longest heritage railway in the UK and a major tourist attraction in North Wales. Using powerful narrow gauge steam locomotives it offers a spectacular 25 mile journey through the heart of the Snowdonia National Park, past lakes and beneath Snowdon, then through picturesque Beddgelert.

It owes its origins to several separate narrow gauge railway initiatives during the 19th and early 20th centuries, primarily to serve local slate quarries. In 1922 the Welsh Highland Railway was formed from the merger of two companies and work began to construct missing links, which enabled the opening of the railway between Dinas, just south of Caernarfon, to Porthmadog in 1923. It faced difficulties from the beginning. The slate industry was in decline and passenger traffic was competing with new road transport. The Ffestiniog Railway took over its management in 1934 but by 1937 all traffic had ceased. Most of the railway was dismantled during World War II.

However the trackbed remained and there began a long and controversial campaign to restore the railway and extend it to Caernarfon. Eventually the Ffestiniog Railway Company took responsibility for the restoration and the line was completed in 2011.

This book provides the opportunity to explore on foot the stunning scenery and history of the varied landscape the railway passes through. It offers 32 circular or linear walks from or between stations, which can be combined with a train ride. The routes, which range from a simple riverside stroll to an exhilarating mountain ridge walk, follow public rights of way, permissive paths or cross Open Access land. They include Lôn Gwyrfai and Lôn Eifion recreational trails, and the former Bryngwyn Branch railway line.

There are walks along the coast, around the fortified walled town of Caernarfon, a World Heritage Site, and the former slate port of Porthmadog. Others take you through the beautiful Aberglaslyn Pass, hidden upland valleys and woodland, past old slate quarries and across foothills offering great views, including Snowdon itself. Many walks are never far from the railway, sometimes alongside it, offering great views of the steam trains. Use the timetable to plan your walks.

Be suitably prepared and equipped, especially on higher routes. Walking boots are recommended, along with appropriate clothing to protect against the elements. The condition of paths can vary according to season and weather. Refer any rights of way problems encountered to Gwynedd Council.

Each walk has a detailed map and descript easily followed, but changes in detail can occu walk is shown on the back cover and a summ; estimated walking time, but allow more time to e country code.

Enjoy your walking!

WALK I

CAERNARFON

DESCRIPTION A 2¼ mile walk exploring the historic old fortified walled town of Caernarfon, a designated World Heritage Site, featuring many places of interest and refreshment options. It combines well with a visit to the impressive castle. Allow about 2 hours.

START Caernarfon station [SH480625]

*C*aernarfon *stands at the mouth of the river Seiont at the western end of The Menai Strait, with easy access to the sea and to nearby Anglesey. The Romans established a fort here, named Segontium, about 79 AD and occupied it for over 300 years. Its main role was to protect the farming and mineral rich lands of Anglesey. It was the largest Roman fort in North Wales and marked the western frontier of the Roman Empire. In the late 11thC the Normans built a motte and bailey castle here, which was then used as one of the courts of the Welsh Princes of Gwynedd.*

The town as we see it today was founded in the late 13thC after Edward I's conquest of Wales. The castle, built on the site of the earlier motte and bailey fortification is one of the most impressive of a chain of coastal castles built to consolidate his control over the traditional Welsh Princes' heartland of North Wales. Work started on the castle and town walls in 1283, but was not completed until 1322. The walls, with eight towers and two gatehouses, encircled a new town laid out in a regular grid pattern of streets, and were designed to protect its English inhabitants. The castle became a seat of government and a Royal palace.

The 'bailey' or small hill of the 11thC castle became part of Castle Green, now Castle Square (Y Maes). Since the late 13thC it has hosted weekly markets and at one time bull-baiting and cockfighting. The hill was taken down and its soil used to create Slate Quay in 1817. Caernarfon then became a bustling port exporting roofing slate transported by rail from inland quarries.

I From the station by the roundabout cross to the building opposite (Caernarfon Trust Buoy Shed) and go past its end to the quayside overlooking the river Seiont and small harbour. Walk along its edge past Slate Quay car park towards the castle, taking care not to trip over any mooring chains. At its end go across Aber swing bridge. *Ferries operated across the river's mouth until 1900 when a road bridge was built. In 1974 it was replaced with Aber bridge.*

2 Turn LEFT for a classic view across the river to the castle. Return across the bridge and turn LEFT. Go past The Anglesey pub and along the promenade above the shore beneath the town walls soon passing through the arch of Porth-yr-Aur (Golden Gate). Continue along the promenade. *At the corner of the town walls is the rare Jesse window of St Mary's church, incorporated into the walls as the garrison church in 1307 and extensively renovated in the early 19thC. At the anchor of the school ship HMS Conway turn RIGHT, soon with a view of nearby Victoria Dock, then RIGHT through the archway along Church Street past St. Mary's church. Turn LEFT along High Street – the old town's traditional business centre – then LEFT along Market Street through the walls to a road. Turn LEFT then RIGHT along the side of Victoria Dock. It was built in the 1870s in response to the demands of the slate industry, but later went into decline. After a regeneration programme it has become a marina and land developed into a fashionable part of Caernarfon to live and visit, with restaurants, hotels and apartments. Cross a footbridge over a wide slipway – used to pull boats out of the water for repairs, and which pre-dates the dock – then go past the Galeri.*

3 At the dock's corner turn LEFT past the modern Yr Harbr complex to the promenade. First turn LEFT to its end overlooking the dock entrance, then return and continue ahead beneath apartments past a small jetty. At the corner turn RIGHT past the apartments then continue briefly above the shore to a Lôn Menai finger post. Here turn RIGHT into Shell Site car park and walk around its edge to its entrance. Continue ahead along the pavement, past the mini-roundabout, and on beside the road, shortly passing toilets, to reach a T-junction beneath the town walls.

4 Go through the archway ahead – *added in the 19thC to improve access* – into the old walled town. Continue up Northgate Street – *once a street of notoriety for sailors visiting the port (see the plaque on the wall of the 16thC Black Boy Inn).* At crossroads turn RIGHT along High Street, past Market Street, then LEFT up Shirehall Street, passing Gwynedd Council buildings incorporating the town's former jail, to the junction beneath the impressive castle. *To the right is the columned frontage of the former County Hall built in 1863, later a Courthouse.* Turn LEFT past the entrance to the castle and Castle Street, then LEFT along Palace Street – *once boasting 15 inns* – past the old Market Hall (1832). At crossroads turn RIGHT and just before Porth Mawr (Great Gate) – *for centuries the only entrance to the town, accessed by a drawbridge, which was closed during a nightly curfew* – turn RIGHT along Hole-in-the Wall Street beneath the town walls, containing the remains of the Bell Tower. At its end turn LEFT, then LEFT again down the next road beneath the outer town walls to Tal-y-Bont arch. *To your right is a tiny room, once a jail and now used as a chapel.*

5 Go under the arch and up steps to your right beneath Tafarn y Porth. Now turn LEFT along Eastgate Street to Turf Square – *for centuries the site of the town stocks.* At crossroads turn RIGHT to reach Castle Square. Turn RIGHT towards the castle. *The metal balcony jutting out from its end was where Prince Charles greeted the crowds after his controversial investiture as Prince of Wales in 1969.* Continue around the Square passing the statues of David Lloyd George,

the town's former Liberal MP and minister, then Sir Hugh Owen, a leading educationalist. In the corner by Copa descend steps to a road below and follow it LEFT to the station.

3

WALK 2

SEGONTIUM

DESCRIPTION A 2½ mile walk featuring the remains of Segontium Roman Fort (See Walk I for information), a circuit of the Victorian Morfa Common Park, and a return alongside the railway. Allow about 2 hours.

START Caernarfon station [SH480625]

1 From the roundabout by the station cross the road leading to the nearby tunnel and go along the road opposite, then turn RIGHT up a stepped path into the corner of Castle Square. Go past the war memorial ahead, then turn RIGHT along Poole Street past shops and an old fountain. On its bend by the main road go through an underpass ahead and up steps. Turn LEFT beside the one-way road, then continue ahead up the A4085 (Beddgelert) and on past the fort to its entrance (free).

2 Afterwards cross the A4085 and go down a nearby surfaced enclosed path to a road. Turn LEFT then RIGHT along Cae Ymryson. Follow the road through the housing estate past Hendre chip shop. At the end of houses continue along Ffordd Eryri past a football pitch, then go down a signposted path on the right by the first house. At a cross-path turn RIGHT a few yards, then take a path on the left down through trees to a road overlooking a lake. Follow it to a T-junction and a nearby gate into Morfa Common Park.

3 Follow instructions in paragraph 3 of Walk 3.

WALK 3

MOOR COMMON PARK

DESCRIPTION A 2¼ mile walk featuring an early 19thC river bridge, a circuit of the Victorian Morfa Common Park, and a return alongside the railway. Allow about 1½ hours.

START Caernarfon station [SH480625]

CAERNARFON
Walk 1
Walk 1
Castle
Slate Quay
P
Station
A4085
Segontiu
Fort
Coed Helen
WALK 3
Lôn Gwyrfai
N
Welsh Highland Railway
WALK 2
Afon Seiont
G
G
Morfa Comm Park
lake
A499

1 Follow instructions in paragraph 1 of Walk 1.

2 Turn LEFT and follow the minor road to a T- junction. Cross the road then the

4

nearby A487 by a designated crossing point. Follow the signposted Lôn Gwyrfai across a former road bridge (1835) over the river, then ahead along a road to the entrance to Morfa Common Park by the driveway to Eryri Hospital.

3 Folllow surfaced paths on an anti-clockwise walk around this small public park and artificial lake, created in the 19thC, turning left at a children's play area. Afterwards take the signposted Lôn Gwyrfai opposite the junction down through trees, under the road bridge and up to a gated crossing of the railway. Follow it back to the station platform.

WALK 4

St Baglan's church, dating from the 13thC, is a rare example of a small medieval church, still containing its original 18thC furnishings. It is now owned by the Friends of Friendless Churches charity and looked after by local people.

I At Bontnewyd Halt use the nearby gated railway crossing then descend a path to the road. Follow it under the railway bridge and on to crossroads. Go along the no through road opposite. After it bends right take a signposted path along Tan y Graig's access track. Before the house cross a ladder-stile on the right, then follow a path angling left up the field to pass above the house to a ladder-stile/gap. Follow the path through the field to a kissing gate, then along the next large field edge to a ladder-stile. Go across the next field up to the church then down to a road adjoining Gwyrfai estuary.

WALK 4
ST BAGLAN'S CHURCH

DESCRIPTION A 4 mile linear walk **(A)** combined with a short train ride, featuring the remote Grade I listed medieval St Baglan's church and extensive coastal views. After alighting at Bontnewydd Halt the route heads west on quiet country roads and field paths to the ancient church. It then follows a scenic minor road along the beautiful Gwyrfai estuary and the Menai Strait on a section of the Wales Coast Path, later crossing the Afon Seiont to Caernarfon castle. Allow about 2½ hours. An alternative 1¾ mile walk **(B)** is to return alongside the railway on the Lôn Eifion trail, which can also be followed from Caernarfon to make a 6 mile circular walk.
START Bontnewydd Halt [SH 479601]
DIRECTIONS From Caernarfon station, near Slate Quay car park, take the train to Bontnewydd Halt – a request stop so please notify the guard before boarding the train.

2 Follow it north, shortly bending along the edge of the Menai Strait past boat launching areas and the Royal Town Golf Club to the mouth of the river opposite Caernarfon Castle. Cross Aber swing bridge, then walk along the edge of Slate Quay car park.

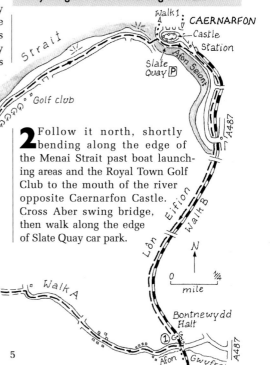

1 From the platform go up steps and across the footbridge into the large car park. At its entrance cross the road and turn LEFT, then go up a narrow road signposted to Rhosgadfan. Later, at a junction, go along a narrow road ahead. At its end by the entrance to Bryn Mair go through the gate ahead and along a track, keeping to its left fork. At the gated entrance to Dwr-yr-Cwm go through another gate ahead.

2 Follow an enclosed path then a walled green track, soon steadily descending and becoming a path to reach a road at a house entrance. Follow it down to cross a bridge over the former Bryngwyn Branch Railway (1877-1937). A little further go through a kissing gate on the left and follow a path through trees to the old railway trackbed. Follow it under the road bridge and on a kissing gate to join a nearby road by Tryfan Crossing.

3 Follow the road across the railway then beside it, shortly bending away to its end at Gwredog-isaf. Continue along a track down a small wooded valley to cross a bridge over the Afon Gwyrai. Go up the road, then at a

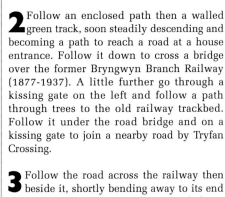

6

junction turn LEFT to a gate. Now follow the enclosed Lôn Gwyrfa trail to Plas Glan Yr Afon. Go through the farm and along its access track past the entrances to Ceunant and Ty Gwyn. Continue along the hedge/tree-lined track. (For **Walk B** continue along the track, then narrow road down to a junction. Go up the minor road opposite and down to a T-junction. Turn left down to the A487, then right along the roadside walkway. The Lôn Gwyrfai crosses a former 1835 road bridge over the river Seion, then follows a road ahead. Soon it turns left, opposite the driveway to Eryri Hospital, down through trees, under the road bridge and up to a gated crossing of the railway, before continuing beside it.)

4 Go through a gate on the left opposite an old iron gate. Go across the field and through a waymarked gateway. Turn RIGHT along the field edge to a ladder-stile. Go up the next large field to a ladder-stile in the left-hand corner and an iron ladder-stile beyond. Go along the field edge to another ladder-stile, then follow a gated path between boundaries, later descending to a house and continuing above the Afon Gwyrfai to another. Go past Pandy Bach ahead and up to a narrow road. Follow it left to The Newborough Arms in Bontnewydd. Turn RIGHT along the main road then cross with care to a road opposite, signposted to Lôn Eifion. Follow the road past the school and out of the village. Just before a bridge, turn RIGHT up a path to cross the railway by Bontnewydd Halt. Follow the Lôn Eifion beside the railway to Caernarfon station.

WALK 5

WAUNFAWR TO CAERNARFON

DESCRIPTION A 6½ mile (**A**) or 5½ mile (**B**) linear walk between Waunfawr and Caernarfon stations. The route rises from the valley by minor road, then crosses an attractive upland area, before descending to follow a railway path to Tryfan Junction. After briefly accompanying the railway it crosses the Afon Gwyrfai, then follows the Lôn Gwyrfai recreational trail past 17thC Plas Glan Yr Afon. Walk A continues west on paths to Bontnewydd, then follows the Lôn Eifion trail beside the railway to Caernarfon. Walk B continues north west with the Lôn Gwyrfai by track and minor roads to join the railway's final section. Allow about 4 and 3 hours respectively. The walks can be shortened by 2 miles by alighting at Tryfan Junction – a request stop – joining the nearby road and following instructions from paragraph 3.
START Waunfawr station [SH 527588]
DIRECTIONS From Caernarfon take the train to Waunfawr.

WALK 6

LÔN EIFION

DESCRIPTION An easy level 2¾ mile (**A**) linear walk in either direction combining a short train ride between Caernarfon and Dinas stations with a walk back on the adjoining Lôn Eifion trail. At Caernarfon the Lôn Eifion starts from the southern end of the platform. At Dinas a request stop – it is accessed from the southern end of the station.
START Caernarfon station [SH480625] or Dinas station [SH 477 587]

*T*he Lôn Eifion and the Welsh Highland Railway share the trackbed of the former Caernarfon-Afonwen standard gauge railway (1867-1964) between Caernarfon and Dinas. It was the first section of the narrow gauge railway to be opened in 1997.

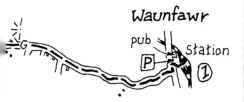

WALK 7

BONTNEWYDD TO DINAS

DESCRIPTION A 7¼ mile meandering walk from Bontnewydd Halt via Tryfan Junction to Dinas station. From Bontnewydd village the route follows paths, then a section of the Lôn Gwyrfai trail past 17thC Plas Glan-yr-Afon. After crossing the Afon Gwyrfai, it accompanies the railway to cross it near Tryfan Junction, then heads south on the Snowdonia Slate Trail along the former narrow gauge Bryngwyn Branch Railway passing through Rhostryfan. After following country lanes to Rhos Isaf it takes field paths to Plas Bodaden, where it crosses the railway, later accompanying it on the Lôn Eifion trail to Dinas station. Allow about 4 hours.

START Bontnewydd Halt [SH 479601]

DIRECTIONS Use the car park at Dinas station, accessed along a minor road from the A487, and take a Caernarfon bound train to Bontnewydd Halt – a request stop so please notify the guard before boarding the train.

I Use the nearby gated railway crossing then follow a path down to the road. Follow it LEFT into Bontnewydd past the school to the A487. Cross with care to the pavement opposite and turn RIGHT. At The Newborough Arms turn LEFT along a narrow road, then shortly follow a signposted path down a lane on the right to the entrance of Dol Pandy farm. Go past Pandy Bach to a gate ahead by another house, then follow a path above the Afon Gwyrfai to a gate by a house. The enclosed path rises through trees to a gate, then continues between walls to a kissing gate, then bends left to another and continues to a ladder-stile. Go along a field edge to a ladder-stile and another nearby, then across the field to a further ladder-stile. Go along the next field edge, then turn LEFT through a waymarked gateway. Continue to a gate in the right-hand field corner onto a tree-lined stony track to join the Lôn Gwyrfai.

2 Follow it RIGHT past the entrances to Ty Gwyn and Ceunant to reach Plas Glan-

yr-Afon – *home to peacocks.* Go through the farmyard past outbuildings, to a gate then along a tarmac section of Lôn Gwyrfai to two gates onto the bend of a narrow road where you leave the trail. Turn RIGHT down the road and across a bridge over the Afon Gwyrfai, then go up an improving track to Gwredog-isaf. Continue along its driveway, soon beside the railway, later crossing it near Tryfan Junction.

3 Go along a stony track to a kissing gate and the Slate Trail. Follow the delightful initially tree-lined path along the trackbed of the former Bryngwyn Branch Line – *opened in 1877 by the North Wales Narrow Gauge Railway Company to service slate quarries on the Moel Tryfan plateau. As well as slate and local supplies, it also carried passengers until 1913. Slate transportation then gradually declined and the line closed in 1937.* Later you pass a seat at a great viewpoint before reaching a picnic area at the site of the former Rhostryfan station. Go through gates and the small car park to cross a footbridge and road to a small gate. Continue with the Slate Trail, passing under a small bridge and crossing a footbridge over a stream, to the village road. The kissing gated Slate Trail continues south for one mile across two minor roads, then along the former trackbed through attractive countryside, later passing Cae Haidd, to its end at a minor road. Follow it RIGHT on a steady descent for ½ mile to a junction. Turn RIGHT through the village of Rhos Isaf past side roads to crossroads by the former 1836 chapel.

4 Go briefly along the road on the right to a signposted path at a small gate. Turn RIGHT along the edge of a large reedy field. At its corner turn LEFT to follow a path by the boundary over two streams to an old gate. Continue along an old part tree-lined walled green track to a gate. Go up the enclosed path, then follow a green track beside Plas Bodaden's boundary wall to a gate and bending close to the railway to a track by outbuildings. Follow it RIGHT through gates across the railway and continue along the access lane to a road.

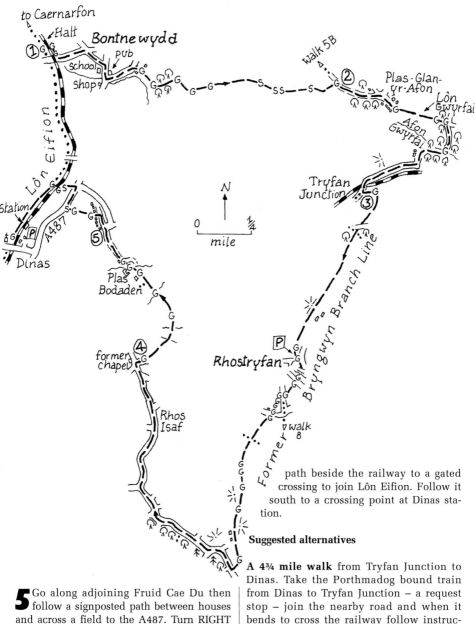

path beside the railway to a gated crossing to join Lôn Eifion. Follow it south to a crossing point at Dinas station.

Suggested alternatives

5 Go along adjoining Fruid Cae Du then follow a signposted path between houses and across a field to the A487. Turn RIGHT along the pavement to a crossing point onto the pavement opposite. Continue to a finger post, descend a short railed iron ladder, then go along the field edge. After a small pool, turn RIGHT to a stile, then follow a short

A 4¾ mile walk from Tryfan Junction to Dinas. Take the Porthmadog bound train from Dinas to Tryfan Junction – a request stop – join the nearby road and when it bends to cross the railway follow instructions from paragraph 3.

A 9¼ mile walk taking the train from Caernarfon to Bontnewydd and extending the walk by returning north along the Lôn Eifion (See Walk 6).

9

WALK 8

MOEL TRYFAN

DESCRIPTION A fascinating 6 mile linear walk between Tyrfan Junction and Waunfawr station, of great industrial interest, panoramic views throughout, two small hilltops, and a micro-brewery pub at the end. The route follows the Snowdonia Slate Trail along the former narrow gauge Bryngwyn Branch railway to Rhostryfan. It then follow field paths to ascend an incline that once linked upland slate quarries at Moel Tryfan with the railway (See Walk 9 for information). After passing beneath tips on the slopes of Moel Tryfan, it offers a short (optional) 300ft/ 90 metres climb to its top (1400 ft/427 metres). It then follows a delightful former tramway offering superb views, then continues across Uwchgwyrfai Common. After a short climb across Moel Smytho (1125 ft/343 metres), it descends by path and road to Waunfawr station. Allow about 3½ hours.

START Tryfan Junction [SH 501591]

DIRECTIONS The large car park of the Snowdon Parc pub on the A4085 at the southern edge of Waunfawr is available for Welsh Highland Railway passengers. A footbridge gives access to the station. Take the Caernarfon bound train to Tryfan Junction – a request stop – so please notify the guard before boarding the train.

I After alighting at Tryfan Junction join the nearby road and when it bends to cross the railway go along a stony track ahead to a kissing gate to join the Slate Trail. Follow the delightful initially tree-lined path along the trackbed of the former Bryngwyn Branch Line, later passing a seat at a great viewpoint, to a picnic area at the site of the former Rhostryfan station. Go through gates and the small car park to cross a footbridge and road to a small gate. Continue with the Slate Trail, passing under a small bridge and across a footbridge over a stream and on to a kissing gate at the village road. Go through a kissing gate opposite and continue to a narrow road. Follow it LEFT up to a junction by cottages.

2 Follow a signposted path up nearby Ffermd Cae Odyn's access track to cross a stile by a gate on the right. Turn LEFT up the field edge to steps by an old gateway. Pass beneath the outbuilding to a small gate, then between boundaries. At a facing wall turn LEFT up a path, soon moving away from the fence and continuing up to a kissing gate in the wall ahead. *Pause to look back at the extensive views.* Follow the wall on your right – *with views of Rhosgadfan, Moel Tryfan, and Moel Eilio.* Just beyond the wall corner turn RIGHT along a stony track, soon bending to a gate. Walk a few yards towards the house then turn RIGHT between walls, soon bending LEFT to a gate. Go up the field to a kissing gate by a pylon and another kissing gate ahead. Go across the tussocky field under power cables to join the boundary on the left, which you follow to a kissing gate by a track. Follow it LEFT – *with a view of slate tips at Moel Tryfan* – past houses to a road. Go down the road.

3 After crossing a low bridge over a stream turn LEFT to follow telegraph poles up the remains of an old incline past cottages. At the top turn RIGHT to nearby slate steps giving access to the road above. Follow it RIGHT past a cottage, then turn LEFT on a signposted path up a wide road towards the slate tips. After passing an information board on the Bryncyn incline, with the remains of Drumhead nearby, the road becomes a wide stony track. Continue along it to where it splits beneath a tip. The Right of Way goes along the left fork and passes a house, but there is now a signed courtesy path avoiding it. Follow it to a small gate, then between a wall and a fence up to join the public footpath. Go through an iron gate and up a path beneath tips past a nearby house, soon bending down to continue along its access track to a minor road. Go along it, then just past Maen Gwyn cottage, turn RIGHT on a signposted path up a stony track, passing between dwellings and bending left to gates. After a kissing gate ahead turn RIGHT up the path near the wall to a narrow cross-track beneath Moel Tryfan. Follow it LEFT to a junction of tracks.

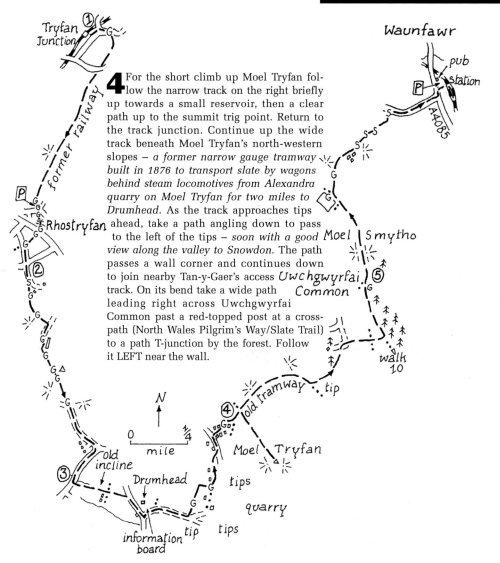

4 For the short climb up Moel Tryfan follow the narrow track on the right briefly up towards a small reservoir, then a clear path up to the summit trig point. Return to the track junction. Continue up the wide track beneath Moel Tryfan's north-western slopes – *a former narrow gauge tramway built in 1876 to transport slate by wagons behind steam locomotives from Alexandra quarry on Moel Tryfan for two miles to Drumhead*. As the track approaches tips ahead, take a path angling down to pass to the left of the tips – *soon with a good view along the valley to Snowdon*. The path passes a wall corner and continues down to join nearby Tan-y-Gaer's access track. On its bend take a wide path leading right across Uwchgwyrfai Common past a red-topped post at a cross-path (North Wales Pilgrim's Way/Slate Trail) to a path T-junction by the forest. Follow it LEFT near the wall.

5 Soon after passing a kissing gate in it take a stony path angling LEFT up the heather covered slope of Moel Smytho to a large boulder on its summit. The path now descends to a waymark post at a wall corner. Keep ahead beside the wall to a gate in it. Here follow a path angling RIGHT to a small gate in a wall. A good path descends the hillside towards Waunfawr, soon passing ruins and going through a wall gap to a stile. It descends via two old ladder-stiles, then through trees and continues to a road which takes you to the A4085 near the car park and well earned refreshments at the Snowdon Parc.

MOEL TRYFAN QUARRY

DESCRIPTION A 6 mile walk, offering extensive views, exploring the hidden upland Uwchgwyrfai Common and its industrial past, with a micro-brewery pub at the end. It follows a path up to the Common, then heads south through its extensive area of heath to former slate quarries on the slopes of Moel Tryfan. This outward section is part of both the waymarked Snowdonia Slate Trail (SST) and North Wales Pilgrim's Way (NWPW). The return route features views into the vast deep Moel Tryfan quarry, a delightful section of a 19thC tramway, and an easy climb up Moel Smytho for panoramic all-round views. Allow about 3½ hours.

START Waunfawr station [SH 527588]

DIRECTIONS The station adjoins the Snowdon Parc pub on the A4085, on the southern outskirts of Waunfawr. The pub's large car park is available for walkers arriving by car. Please enjoy refreshments at the pub upon return.

*W**hilst** other slate quarries in the area developed quickly during the 19thC, the upland quarries on the Moel Tryfan plateau were initially restricted by isolation, transportation problems and disputes. This all changed with the opening of the Bryngwyn branch of the North Wales Narrow Gauge Railway in 1877. Slate from the quarries was moved to Drumhead and down an incline to Bryngwyn station, then taken by rail to Dinas, where it was transferred onto the LNWR line for its journey to Caernarfon for shipping far and wide. The Moel Tryfan quarry, which first opened in 1800, became profitable, with 150 men employed In 1890. In 1918 the quarry merged with the adjoining Alexandra and Cilgwyn quarries. Rock falls were always a problem but extraction of slate continued until 1972, and has recently restarted.*

I From the car park entrance, accessed by footbridge from the station, cross the road and turn LEFT then go up a narrow road

signposted to Rhosgadfan. Shortly, cross a ladder-stile signposted Y Fron/SST/NWPW. Go along an old green track, soon becoming a path which continues through bracken, then rises steadily through trees to an old iron ladder-stile and on up to another. The path continues up the open hillside beside the wall to a stile, then rises to a waymarked wall gap and past three small ruins. It continues up to a small gate in the wall onto a junction of paths on Uwchgwyrfai Common.

2 Take the one heading half-LEFT across heather to an old iron gate in a wall and follow the waymarked path LEFT beside it. At its corner turn RIGHT with the SST/NWPW. The path soon angles away from the wall across heather, becomes less distinct, passes a walled enclosure and a house, then joins its access track. Follow it to cottages, then continue along a narrow road past Hafod Ruffydd farm – *with a view ahead of the slate quarry tips on Moel Tryfan.* On its bend by Tan-y-Gaer's access track turn LEFT along a wide path on the SST/NWPW across the Common, soon taking its right fork to a red-topped post at a crossroad of paths. Follow the wide path ahead south through the expansive heather towards Mynydd Fawr and Snowdon. Later the trails bend round the end of a small gully (old workings) and continues south – *now with a good view of the Nantlle ridge ahead* – past the end of the forest below, with old tips now encroaching from the right, over a cross path, to reach a crossroad of paths.

3 Here turn RIGHT with the SST/NWPW passing the left side of the nearby large slab of rock. Follow the waymarked path up to a good viewpoint near a large depression – *all that remains of former waterworks* – and across the hillside – *soon with a view down to Llyn Nantlle Uchaf beneath the Nantlle ridge* – to an old tip. The path then bends right between it and a smaller one to a slate quarry road. Follow it LEFT. When it bends left go along the old green track ahead to a T-junction just before the quarry. Turn RIGHT along the track, then just after it bends right do a sharp U-turn LEFT along an old track towards the quarry.

4 Now turn RIGHT to follow a narrow green track past the side of a nearby fenced-off old quarry hole. It then rises steadily by the perimeter fence overlooking the vast quarry beneath Moel Tryfan's rocky summit. Soon after levelling out at the fence corner the now wide path crosses an old spoil heap to join a stony track below by old quarry buildings. The track descends past a good view down into the Moel Tryfan quarry, with its small pools. After a brief descent the wide slate track passes a large flat area of the former Alexandra (Cors y Briniau) quarry (1862-1934) and the end of the fence, marking the northern end of the Moel Tryfan quarry. Take the track's left fork, now the former Alexandra quarry tramway, bending LEFT across an exposed embanked section overlooking the valley. The former tramway continues between spoil tips, soon on a gentle descent. *The narrow gauge tramway was built in 1876 and ran for two miles from Drumhead gaining height gradually. Wagons were pulled by small steam locomotives.*

5 At the end of the last tip on the right take a path down beneath it, and on past a wall corner below to join Tan-y-Gaer's access track. On its bend take a wide path leading RIGHT across the Common, soon crossing your outward route at the red-topped post to reach a path T- junction by the forest. Follow it LEFT near the wall. Soon after passing a kissing gate in it take a stony path angling LEFT up the heather covered slope of Moel Smytho to a large boulder on its summit, then down across its northern slope to a familiar wall corner. Return along your outward route.

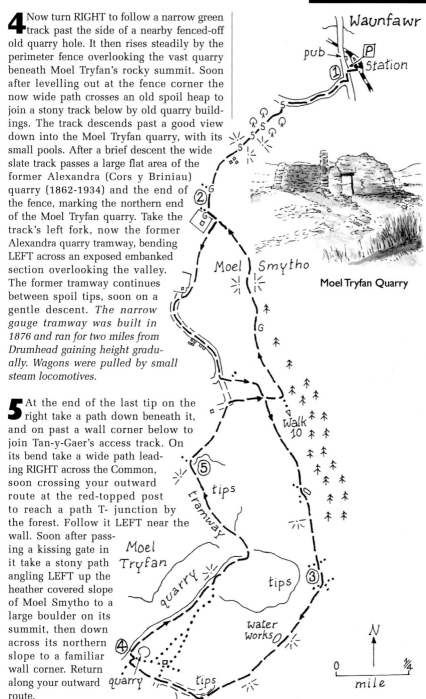

Moel Tryfan Quarry

AROUND CWM GWYRFAI

DESCRIPTION A varied 5 mile walk around the Gwyrfai Valley. The route first rises, with increasingly good views, to hidden upland Uwchgwyrfai Common, then makes an easy climb across the small heather-covered hill of Moel Smytho (1125 ft/343 metres), offering extensive all-round views. It continues south along the forested edge of the Common, then descends a waymarked path to Betws Garmon in the valley before returning by field paths and minor road to Waunfawr. Allow about 3 hours.
START Waunfawr station [SH 527588]
DIRECTIONS The station adjoins the Snowdon Parc pub car park on the A4085, on the southern outskirts of Waunfawr. The large car park is available for walkers arriving by car. Please enjoy refreshments at the micro brewery pub in return.

Waunfawr had a station on the North Wales Narrow Gauge Railway which opened in 1877 to carry dressed slate to Dinas Junction. The station was reopened in 2000. Uwchgwyrfai Common extends from urban fringes up to the summit of Mynydd Mawr. It includes a large area of heath and is associated with famous Welsh author Dr Kate Roberts, who lived in nearby Rhosgadfan

I From the platform go up steps and across the footbridge into the large car park. At its entrance cross the road and turn LEFT then go up a narrow road signposted to Rhosgadfan. Shortly, cross a ladder-stile signposted Y Fron/Snowdonia SlateTrail/North Wales Pilgrim's Way. Go along an old green track, soon becoming a path which continues through bracken, then rises steadily through trees to an old iron ladder-stile and on up to another. The path continues up the open hillside beside the wall to a stile then rises to a waymarked wall gap and past three small ruins to eventually reach a small gate in the wall onto a junction of paths on

Uwchgwyrfai Common. Take the one heading half-LEFT across heather to an old iron gate in a wall. Follow the waymarked path LEFT beside the wall.

2 At its corner, where the trails turn right, follow a good path ahead up through heather to a large boulder on the summit of Moel Smytho – *offering views of Mynydd Mawr, Snowdon, Moel Eilio, Nantle ridge, Moel Tryfan, The Rivals, Anglesey and Caernarfon Castle.* The stony path descends to the perimeter wall of a cleared forest. Follow a narrow path close to the wall past a kissing gate in it, then later a section of mature forest. At its end continue near the boundary to a kissing gate in it at a finger post.

3 The path descends, soon above a stream in a gully, then moves away, passes a small ruin, and descends to an old small gateway at a forest corner. The path goes briefly down its edge and bends into the dark forest then angles half-RIGHT down through conifers past a section of wall. A few yards further, just below a large boulder, red arrows on trees indicate that you turn LEFT across the stream/gully. Ignore a waymark wrongly pointing right suggesting the path continues ahead down through the trees. (I have reported this to Gwynedd Council, so hopefully a correct waymark will be in place.) The path crosses the conifer-covered slope to a waymark post in the bottom forest corner. The path descends through deciduous trees and follows a wall to a small gate, then descends the edge of a field to a waymarked gateway. It continues down through reeds and above a stream, soon crossing it to reach a kissing gate and a narrow road. Go down the road past Bwthyn Tyddyn Bach to a kissing gate on the bend by other houses.

4 Follow the wide path down the field, in its corner bending to a kissing-gate near the Afon Gwyrfai. The path continues to a long footbridge over the river and a kissing gate beyond into Bryn Gloch Caravan & Camping Park. Go half-LEFT to follow a lane through the caravan field to the site access road. Turn LEFT along it, at a junction bending RIGHT to cross over the Welsh Highland Railway. Bend LEFT a few yards then turn RIGHT on the waymarked path between buildings to a kissing gate by the A4085 at Betws Garmon. Cross with care to reach the nearby small mid 19thC church.

5 Follow an enclosed path through the graveyard, then along a field edge. At the churchyard corner the waymarked path heads

[Map with labels: Waunfawr, Walks 12 & 13, Afon, Gwyrfai, pub, P, Station, A4085, N, 0 ¼ mile, Tyn-yr-onnen, Garreg Fawr, Ty-isaf, old tramway, Betws Garmon, Bryn Gloch, Afon Gwyrfai, Moel Smytho, Uwchgwyrfai, Walks 9 & 11, Common]

in it. The waymarked path now heads up to a small iron gate by Ty-isaf, now sadly a ruin. *This early 19thC smallholder's cottage, with integral cowhouse is Grade II listed. Its occupants likely derived a living from farming and work in the slate quarry.*

6 The path now follows a wall on the left to a kissing gate, continues beneath wooded Garreg Fawr past a small ruin, then along the field edge to a small gate. Go ahead along the next field past old concrete structures to a kissing gate and another beyond. Go half-LEFT to a waymark post then along a field edge to a kissing gate onto a narrow road. Follow it LEFT past

half-LEFT along the edge of a large field to a kissing gate and across the next field, crossing the line of an old tramway. *It once linked the Garreg Fawr slate quarry above, which opened in 1802 and operated intermittently until the 1930s, to the North Wales Narrow Gauge Railway (later the Welsh Highland Railway). On the old quarry stands an unusual Grade II listed castellated engine house.* At a gateway turn RIGHT alongside the wall to a kissing gate

Tyn-yr-onnen Caravan Park into the outskirts of Waunfawr. After passing a signposted Slate Trail path on the right, go through a kissing gate on the left at the entrance to Gwernydd, opposite terraced bungalows. Follow the narrow enclosed path down to the A4085. Cross the road with care then follow it LEFT across the bridge over the river, then another over the Welsh Highland Railway to the start.

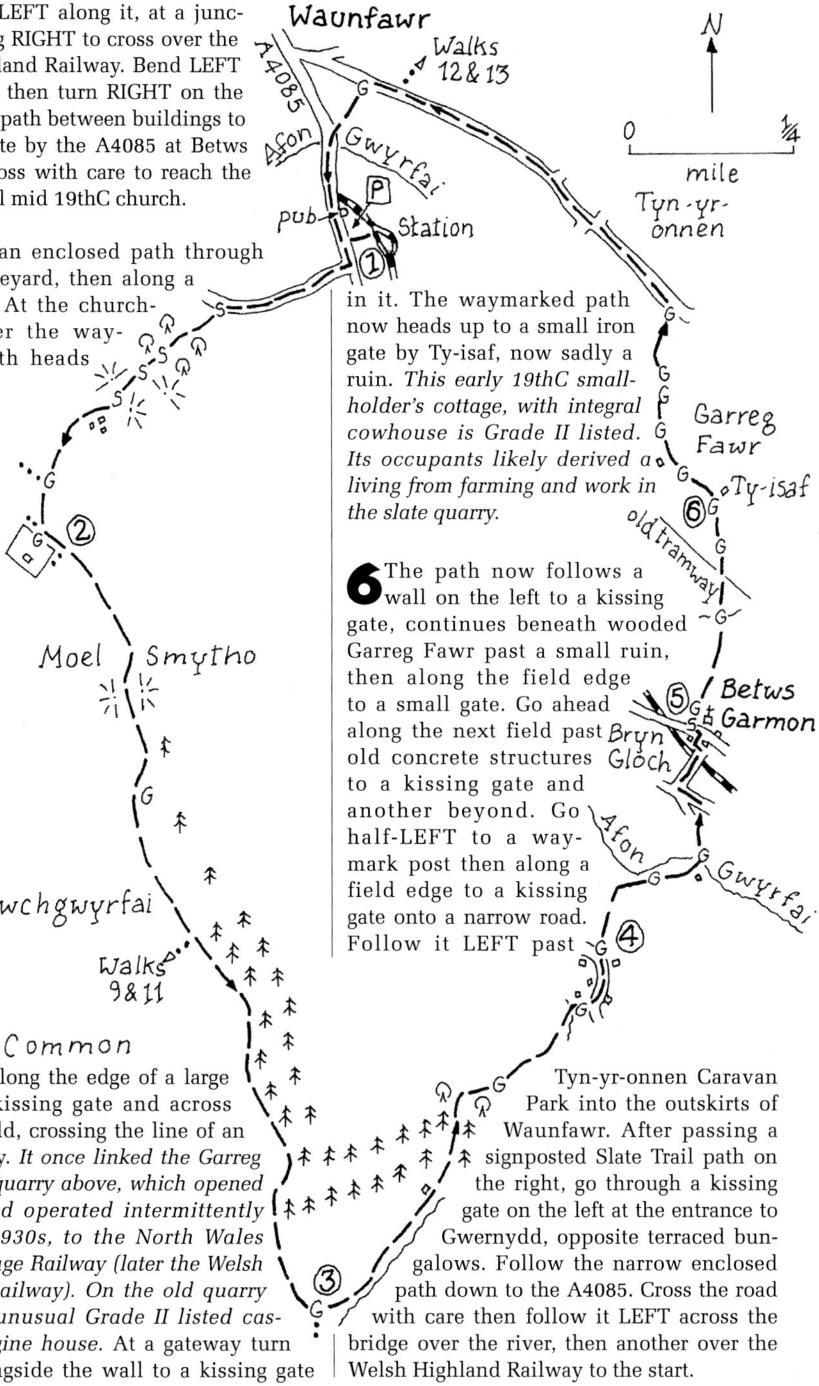

MOEL SMYTHO

DESCRIPTION A 3½ mile walk exploring Uwchgwyrfai Common's large area of upland heath associated with famous Welsh author Dr Kate Roberts, who lived in nearby Rhosgadfan, and a micro-brewery pub at its end. It follows a section of the Snowdonia Slate Trail/North Wales Pilgrim's Way up to the Common, then makes an easy climb onto Moel Smytho (1125 ft/343 metres), offering extensive all-round views. After meandering around the Common it descends the same way. Allow about 2 hours.
START Waunfawr station [SH 527588] See Walk 10.

1 From the platform cross the footbridge into the large car park. At its entrance cross the road and turn LEFT then go up a narrow road signposted to Rhosgadfan. Shortly, cross a ladder-stile signposted Y Fron/SST/NWPW. The path soon rises steadily through trees to an old iron ladder-stile and on up to another. It heads up the open hillside beside a wall to a stile, then rises to a waymarked wall gap and passes three small ruins. It continues up to a small gate in the wall onto a junction of paths on Uwchgwyrfai Common.

2 Take the one heading half-LEFT across heather to an old iron gate in a wall. Follow the waymarked path LEFT beside the wall. At its corner, where the trails turn right, follow a good path ahead up through heather to a large boulder on the summit of Moel Smytho. The stony path continues down to the perimeter wall of a cleared forest. Follow a narrow path close to the wall past a kissing gate in it.

3 Later, at a kink in the wall before the mature forest, turn RIGHT along another path, then at a crossroad of paths at a waymark post turn RIGHT, now back on the SST/NWPW, soon bending to a road. Follow it RIGHT past Hafod Ruffydd farm and cottages, then continue along a track.

At its end at a house turn LEFT and follow a path near the wall, round its corner and on past its next one.

4 Take its right fork up to join a wall, soon enclosed by another, to reach an information board on Uwchgwyrfai Common. Join a nearby cottage's access track, soon descending to a road at a popular viewpoint. Turn RIGHT a few yards then take a track on the right to another at the entrance to Ty Newydd. Turn RIGHT up it to its end at gated entrance to Penrallt. Continue ahead up a wide path near the wall, later keeping with the left fork to each the gate at point 2. Follow your outward path down to the start.

WALK 12

HAFOD OLEU

DESCRIPTION An enjoyable 2¾ mile walk on waymarked local trails exploring an area above Waunfawr known as Hafod Oleu. The route rises steadily to a scenic minor road, then visits nearby Open Access land for extensive views, before returning down to Antur Waunfawr, a Social Enterprise organization, with its enticing Blas y Waun café (*Open Mon-Fri 10 -4*). Allow about 2 hours.

START Waunfawr station [SH 527588] See Walk 13.

Waunfawr's most famous son was John Evans (1770-99), who had a short but eventful life. Born in the village he later lived in a single storey cottage at Hafod Oleu. Driven by tales of legendary Welsh speaking Indians he travelled to America, where he worked for the Spanish Crown, exploring and mapping the Missouri river, and living among the Mandan tribe.

1 From the platform cross the footbridge into the large car park. At its entrance turn RIGHT with care along the road past the Snowdon Parc pub, over the railway and the Afon Gwyrfai, then go along a narrow enclosed path up to a road. Follow it RIGHT then turn LEFT along a signposted narrow path up past a lane to a narrow road by Cartrefle. Go up the nearby waymarked walled Hafod Oleu path ahead to a kissing gate and along a reedy field to another. Go past the barn and along the field edge to a wide gap in the corner and a hidden kissing gate beyond. Follow the path between a wall and a stream up to a kissing gate, then go up a lane.

2 On its bend keep ahead beside a low wall, soon bending right through a gap in its corner. Continue beside another wall, across a large footbridge over a stream and on to join an access track. When it becomes two green tracks go up the one ahead passing a nearby old cottage. It soon bends left and rises to a gate, then continues above a stream up to a cross-track. Turn LEFT through a gate, over the stream and on past cottages up to a minor road.

3 Go up the road then along a stony track signposted to Pendas Eithin. At the entrance to the cottage keep ahead beside the wall. At its corner turn LEFT down a path and past a wall corner to a cross-path 10 yards above a facing wall. Follow it LEFT to a wall corner then angle RIGHT down a path to the road. After the cattle grid turn LEFT along the access track to Dinas. Go past the house to a kissing gate on the bend. Go along the field edge to go through a small gate.

4 Go down the field edge to a kissing gate, through trees and down the edge of two fields to a kissing gate. The path continues down to a small gate, then an enclosed section to a road. Follow it RIGHT past cottages, then at Llys Awel turn LEFT along a enclosed path to another road. Follow it LEFT down to Antur Waunfawr and its café. Continue past the side road then go along the no through road ahead to join your outward route.

WALK 13

CEFN DDU

DESCRIPTION A 6 mile figure of eight walk, offering panoramic views, to the top of Cefn Ddu (1446 ft/441 metres), from whose western slopes were transmitted the first ever morse code wireless message to Australia in 1918. The route follows waymarked trails up through the fields of Hafod Oleu to a minor road at a good viewpoint. It continues across the heather covered lower slopes of Cefn Ddu before rising steadily with a fence to a trig point on its summit. It descends through an old slate quarry, before heading west on tracks, then scenic upland road to descend the local waymarked trail to Antur Waunfawr and its café. Allow about 4 hours. Avoid in poor visibility.

START Waunfawr station [SH 527588]

DIRECTIONS The station adjoins the Snowdon Parc pub car park on the A4085, on the southern outskirts of Waunfawr. The large car park is available for walkers arriving by car. Please enjoy refreshments at the micro brewery pub in return.

Waunfawr had a station on the North Wales Narrow Gauge Railway which opened in 1877 to carry dressed slate to Dinas Junction. The station was reopened in 2000 as part of the Welsh Highland Railway reconstruction. People in the village lived off the land and from work in local quarries.

From the platform go up steps and cross the footbridge into the large car park. At its entrance turn RIGHT with care along the road past the Snowdon Parc pub, over the railway and the Afon Gwyrfai, then go along a narrow enclosed path up to a road. Follow it RIGHT then turn LEFT along a signposted narrow path up past a lane to a narrow road by Cartrefle. Go up the nearby waymarked walled Hafod Oleu path ahead to a kissing gate and along a reedy field to another. Go past the barn and along the field edge to a wide gap in the corner and a hidden kissing gate beyond. Follow the path between a wall and a stream up to a kissing gate, then go up a lane.

2 On its bend keep ahead beside a low wall, soon bending right through a gap in its corner. Continue beside another wall, across a large footbridge over a stream and on to join an access track. When it becomes two green tracks go up the one ahead passing a nearby old cottage. It soon bends left and

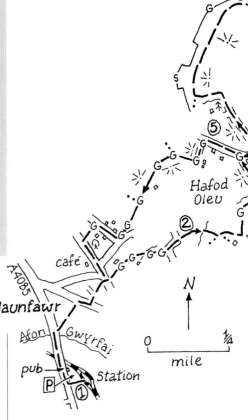

rises to a gate, then continues above a stream up to a cross-track. Turn LEFT through a gate, over the stream and on past cottages up to a minor road.

3 Go up the road then along a stony track signposted to Pendas Eithin. At the entrance to the cottage keep ahead beside the wall. At its corner turn LEFT down a path and past a wall corner to a cross-path 10 yards above a facing wall. Follow it RIGHT across the heather and gorse covered slope,

18

soon taking its rising right fork. The path contours across the hillside to eventually approach a gate in the boundary ahead. *On the other side of the boundary, from 1914-39, extending up the slope of Cefn Du were ten 400 ft steel masts that held a vast aerial* angles RIGHT to join a green track heading west. After a gate follow the now stony track to join another by tips near a forest corner. Follow it past the forest to rejoin a narrow upland road, which continues west beneath quarry tips, later descending past point 3.

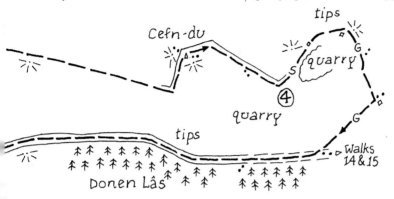

system linked to a Marconi wireless transmitting station located further downhill. Its purpose was to send messages to the USA but it is best known for its historic message to Waroonga Australia in 1921, with no relay stations. Just before the gate turn RIGHT and follow the fence up to a trig point and small ruin on Cefn Du's summit. *Just to the north is a large ruin, once part of the transmitting station system.* Follow a path straight ahead parallel with the nearby fence down towards the distant vast Dinorwic quarry to join a fence/wall which you follow down to its corner.

Trig point on Cefn Ddu

4 Turn LEFT alongside the wall to a slate ladder-stile/gate. Now follow a path along the edge of a vast deep slate quarry – *worked from the 18thC to the early 19thC* – soon bending away down to pass between two small quarry buildings. A few yards beyond the path bends RIGHT down into a quarry, through an area of tips, soon passing to the left of an old building – *with a good view of Llyn Padarn and Llanberis* – then contouring to a small gate in a boundary. Go down a faint green track, past a waymark post, and on with the old reedy track past a wall corner ahead, then beside the wall – *with views of trains on Snowdon.* Just before its end and a building the track

5 After passing two cottages, take a sign-posted path/ Hafod Oleu trail through a kissing gate and down the access lane to Bryn Tirion. Go through a small gate on the right, down the field edge and through a wall gap to a small gate beyond. Go down the field edge to a kissing gate, through trees and down the edge of two fields to a kissing gate. The path continues down to a small gate, then an enclosed section to a road. Follow it RIGHT past cottages, then at Llys Awel turn LEFT along a enclosed path to another road. Follow it LEFT down to Antur Waunfawr and its café. Continue past the side road then on the bend go along the no through road ahead to join your outward route.

WALK 14

BWLCH MAESGWM

DESCRIPTION A splendid 7½ mile linear undulating linear upland walk between Waunfawr and Snowdon Ranger stations, on good paths, bridleways, tracks and scenic upland road, offering great ever changing mountain and lake views. The route follows a waymarked local trail up to a good viewpoint, then heads east by narrow road and stony track to Bwlch y Groes. The delightful track then descends steadily, offering great views down to Llanberis and Llyn Padarn. After crossing the Afon Goch the route follows a bridleway south, with good views of Snowdon and its mountain railway, then along a narrow valley up to Bwlch Maesgwm (1532 ft/467 metres). The bridleway descends to the Snowdon Ranger Path, which it follows down to the station. Allow about 5 hours.

START Waunfawr station [SH 527588]

DIRECTIONS Use the Snowdon Ranger car park adjoining the A4085 near Snowdon Ranger Youth Hostel, then follow the signed Snowdon Ranger Path up to the station platform. This is a request stop so give a clear signal to the engine driver. Take the train to Waunfawr station. Alternatively catch the Sherpa S4 bus.

1-2 Follow instructions in paragraphs 1 & 2 of Walk 13.

3 Go up the road shortly passing between old slate quarry tips and Donen Las Forest. At the road end continue along a stony track. Just after the forest corner continue along the track's right fork past a disused quarry to a kissing gate/gate at Bwlch y Groes.

4 Continue along the track – *enjoying increasingly good views of Dinorwic slate quarry, then down to Llyn Padarn and Llanberis* – shortly descending to a gate. The now old green track descends steadily to a ladder-stile/gate, then continues down to a ruin. Go briefly down the old narrow lane then turn RIGHT along a signposted

bridleway to a bridge over the Afon Goch, then across the hillside to the gated end of a road by a house. The bridleway continues south along the track ahead – *with views of steam trains on Snowdon* – crosses the Afon Hwch, then passes ruins to a gate. After a cottage the narrow stony bridleway rises steadily past ruins, then along the Maesgwm valley, later rising steadily to Bwlch Maesgwm.

5 After a small gate in the wall the bridleway descends to a ladder-stile/gate – *with a view of Llyn-y-gadar and Moel Hebog beyond.* Continue ahead with the bridleway down across the hillside, or alternative path shown, to join the Snowdon Ranger Path. Follow it across the hillside, shortly zig-zagging down to a house with a waterwheel, then descend its access track to cross the railway. Turn LEFT through a gate and along a path to the station and down to the A4085 and car park.

WALK 15

MOEL EILIO

DESCRIPTION An exhilarating 7¼ mile linear mountain walk between Waunfawr and Snowdon Ranger stations, featuring one of the finest grass ridges in Snowdonia, offering extensive views of mountains, coast and Snowdon Mountain Railway. The route follows Walk 14 up to Bwlch y Groes, then climbs steadily up the northern slopes of Moel Eilio to its summit (2381 feet/726 metres). It continues along the undulating ridge to Foel Goch, then descends to Bwlch Maesgwm, to rejoin Walk 14 for a descent to Snowdon Ranger station. Allow about 5 hours. For experienced hill walkers and best avoided in poor visibility.

START Waunfawr station [SH 527588]

DIRECTIONS See Walk 14.

1-2 Follow instructions in paragraphs 1 & 2 of Walk 13.

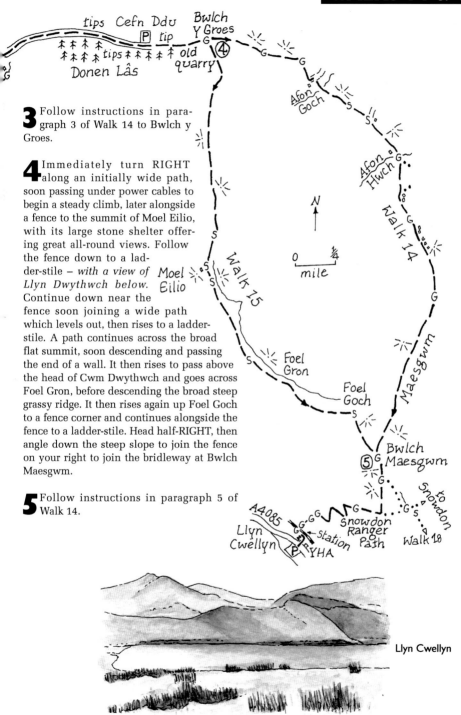

3 Follow instructions in paragraph 3 of Walk 14 to Bwlch y Groes.

4 Immediately turn RIGHT along an initially wide path, soon passing under power cables to begin a steady climb, later alongside a fence to the summit of Moel Eilio, with its large stone shelter offering great all-round views. Follow the fence down to a ladder-stile – *with a view of Llyn Dwythwch below.* Continue down near the fence soon joining a wide path which levels out, then rises to a ladder-stile. A path continues across the broad flat summit, soon descending and passing the end of a wall. It then rises to pass above the head of Cwm Dwythwch and goes across Foel Gron, before descending the broad steep grassy ridge. It then rises again up Foel Goch to a fence corner and continues alongside the fence to a ladder-stile. Head half-RIGHT, then angle down the steep slope to join the fence on your right to join the bridleway at Bwlch Maesgwm.

5 Follow instructions in paragraph 5 of Walk 14.

Llyn Cwellyn

21

WALK 16

BENEATH MYNYDD DRWS-Y-COED

DESCRIPTION A 4 mile walk on good bridleways exploring the varied landscape beneath the imposing mountain of Mynydd Drws-y-coed. The route follows the initial section of the Lôn Gwyrfai, a waymarked shared recreational trail, past Llyn-y-Gader and along the edge of Beddgelert Forest. It then follows a bridleway on tracks through the forest, rising easily in stages to a height of 300 metres, and across the open lower slopes of Mynydd Drws-y-coed, offering extensive views, later descending to rejoin the Lôn Gwyrfai. Allow about 2½ hours.

START Rhyd Ddu station or SNPA car park [SH 571526]

DIRECTIONS The station and car park adjoin the A4085 about 3 miles north of Beddgelert.

I From the northern end of the platform cross the railway line by the water tower to a small gate to reach the car park below. From the car park entrance by toilets cross the road with care to an elaborate iron gate opposite to join the Lôn Gwyrfai. The stony trail heads across reedy terrain towards Mynydd Drws-y-coed, crosses the Afon Gwyrfai and passes your return bridleway. The gated trail then crosses a narrow fenced causeway – *originally used to transport slate by rail* – past Llyn-y-Gader – *to reach the site of the former Gadair-wyllt slate quarry (1885-1920)*. It continues along the edge of the lake – *offering a classic view of Snowdon* – then the edge of Beddgelert Forest, later bending left along a forestry track to a T-junction at post 52. Here you leave the trail by turning RIGHT up the narrow forestry track.

2 When it splits take the one leading right on the waymarked yellow Derwen cycle trail. Shortly, continue with the Derwen trail along the track's older right fork. At post 43 it bends left towards the imposing slopes of Mynydd Drws-y-coed, passing along the open forest edge, then rising steadily. At a

Derwen trail waymark post just before post 42 turn RIGHT up a narrow stony bridleway through trees to an old small gateway in a wall, after which it descends out of the forest to another small gate at a great viewpoint.

3 The bridleway goes across the hillside, crosses a stream, then begins a steady descent – *with a great view down to Llyn-y-Gader and across to Snowdon* – across reedy terrain to a gate. The bridleway contours across the hillside, crosses a stream, then descends to a gate/ladder-stile. It continues down to a bridle gate beyond a stream then follows a fence along the edge of a large reedy area to a gate near a road. Turn RIGHT along the stony bridleway to rejoin the Lôn Gwyrfai back to the start. For refreshments go through the car park to the gated railway crossing and follow a stony track down to the road and walk with care along to either Ty Mawr tea-room or The Cwellyn Arms pub.

WALK 17

AFON COLWYN

DESCRIPTION A 4 mile walk exploring the varied landscape near Rhyd-Ddu, offering good views of Snowdon, other mountains and lakes. The route first follows the initial stony bridleway section of the Snowdon Rhyd-Ddu Path up to a crossroad of bridleways at 1050 feet/320 metres. It then heads south towards Ffridd Uchaf to join a recently created waymarked gated link path following the Afon Colwyn to join the Lôn Gwyrfai recreational trail, returning with it through the edge of Beddgelert Forest and past attractive Llyn-y-Gader. Allow about 2½ hours.

START Rhyd Ddu station or SNPA car park [SH 571526]

DIRECTIONS See Walk 16.

I From the northern end of the platform cross the railway line by the water tower to a small gate to reach the car park below.

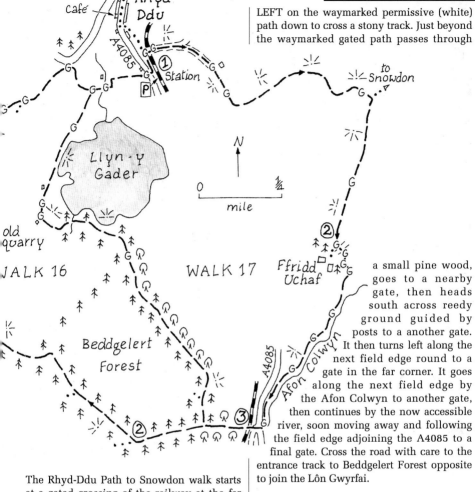

LEFT on the waymarked permissive (white) path down to cross a stony track. Just beyond the waymarked gated path passes through a small pine wood, goes to a nearby gate, then heads south across reedy ground guided by posts to a another gate. It then turns left along the next field edge round to a gate in the far corner. It goes along the next field edge by the Afon Colwyn to another gate, then continues by the now accessible river, soon moving away and following the field edge adjoining the A4085 to a final gate. Cross the road with care to the entrance track to Beddgelert Forest opposite to join the Lôn Gwyrfai.

The Rhyd-Ddu Path to Snowdon walk starts at a gated crossing of the railway at the far end of the car park. Go up the stony track, soon taking its right fork, rising steadily, to gates by a barn. Continue up the wide gravel path to further gates, soon afterwards bending towards Snowdon – *with increasingly good views along Llyn Cwellyn* – and continuing up to another gate. At a crossroad of bridleways, where the Rhyd-Ddu Path turns left through a gate, turn RIGHT along a waymarked bridleway, soon descending to a gate in a wall, then continuing down beside another.

2 Just before a small gate at the corner of a wood above Ffridd Uchaf farm turn

3 Follow the trail signposted to Rhyd-Ddu over the gated railway crossing and up the forestry track. At a junction turn RIGHT, soon taking the track's right fork along the edge of the forest to a small gate then past the edge of Llyn-y-Gader – *offering a classic view of Snowdon*. The trail continues to the site of the former Gadair-wyllt slate quarry (1885-1920) then goes along a narrow causeway – *originally used to transport slate by rail* – past Llyn y Gader then crosses the Afon Gwyrfai to reach the A4085 at Rhyd-Ddu opposite the car park entrance. For refreshments see end of paragraph 3 in Walk 18.

SNOWDON RANGER TO RHYD-DDU

DESCRIPTION A 4 mile linear walk between two stations at popular Snowdon starting points. The route follows the Snowdon Ranger Path to a height of 1246 ft/380 metres. It then takes a well waymarked link path on a long steady descent across reedy terrain, wet in places, via an attractive gorge and the former Glan yr Afon slate quarry, back to Rhyd-Ddu, with its welcoming pub and tea-room. Allow about 3 hours.

START Snowdon Ranger [SH 565551]
DIRECTIONS From Rhyd-Ddu SNPA car park take a train to Snowdon Ranger – a request stop so please notify the guard before boarding the train – or the Sherpa S4 bus. The Snowdon Ranger Path starts from the entrance to Caer Orsaf, opposite the bus stop and rises to the railway halt.

The Snowdon Ranger Path was named after the mountain guide John Morton, known as the 'Snowdon Ranger', who in the early 19thC built an inn on the site of the youth hostel, from where he guided visitors to Snowdon's summit along this route.

After arriving by train join the Snowdon Ranger Path (SRP) from the end of the platform. The path runs beside the line to a gate onto a concrete track, which crosses the railway and rises to a gate. Continue up the stony track past a house with a waterwheel, bending right up to a gate. The SRP now zig-zags up the hillside, levels out then continues across the hillside to a gate by a stream. After a further 30 yards, leave the SRP to cross a ladder-stile on the right.

2 Follow a path across the reedy terrain, soon beginning a long steady descent towards the old slate quarry below, guided by waymark posts, to a footbridge over a stream. Soon the waymarked path bends

right then follows a fence to a ladder-stile in it. The path continues down to cross further streams and a slate track, then descends to a small footbridge over the Afon Treweunydd, tumbling down a valley of slate tips – *with a good view of Llyn Cwellyn.* Cross the ladder-stile above and go down the path then along the base of tips to the top of a section of old incline. Here the path turns LEFT up between tips. After passing old quarry buildings, the waymarked path climbs the tip on the right to an old tramway. It bears RIGHT a few yards then LEFT across the tip and down to a ladder-stile. Continue to another ladder-stile ahead.

3 Ignore the Glastir permissive path angling left but follow the main path down past waymark posts to a stream and on to a waymark post by a small crag. The path continues across the slope to a gap in a wall, then descends to a footbridge over a stream. It goes through another wall gap, descends to a gate, and crosses the railway line to another gate below. Follow the wide gravel path to a T-junction and turn RIGHT. When it splits you have a choice. The left fork takes you to a gate by houses onto a track that leads up to the car park. For refreshments follow the right fork to the road at Rhyd-du with The Cwellyn Arms pub and Ty Mawr tea-room nearby. Afterwards go along the road with care then take a signposted path/stony track on the left between houses up to the car park.

WALK 19

BEDDGELERT

DESCRIPTION A short, enjoyable, 1½ mile circular walk featuring part of the Lôn Gwyrfai recreational trail, three crossings of the railway, woodland and good views of Moel Hebog. Allow about 1½ hours.

START Beddgelert station or car park below [SH 588482]

DIRECTIONS If arriving by car use the car park signposted from the A498 between the Tourist Information Centre and the Royal Goat Hotel. From an information board on Lôn Gwyrfai at the car park corner, go through a gate and up a tarmac path, soon bending past a path rising to the station above to point 2.

Lôn Gwyrfai. Go up the lane past a farm, over the railway and on to a house, after which it becomes a stony track. It rises through tall conifers, crosses the railway again and continues up through mature mixed woodland, then beside the stream to a house and barn. Here you leave the Lôn Gwyrfai which turns right.

3 Turn LEFT across the stream and along a concrete lane past the side of the house. Continue up the track to pass between Cysgod yr Hebog and Beudy Bach and on past a wood corner – *with views of Moel Hebog*. Just before the track begins to descend into woodland at a telegraph pole and facing iron gates, go through the one on the left. Follow a path down the field near the fence. At a waymark post by the corner of a small fenced wood on the left, bend LEFT

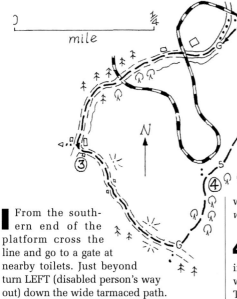

BEDDGELERT

with the path down past the fence corner and on through an old gateway in a wall ahead. Go down the waymarked path – *with the railway line in view*.

4 Do not go through a gateway in the wall, but follow it down to a ladder-stile/old iron gate in its corner. Turn LEFT along the wide path beside the wall to a waymark post. The path continues a little lower than the wall, passes through an old gateway, reaches a kissing gate and crosses a footbridge over the railway. Descend between houses, over the road end and on down a path to a finger post. Turn LEFT through a gate on the signposted Rhyd ddu trail. Follow the stony trail up to the station. For the car park descend steps then a meandering stony path to your outward route.

1 From the southern end of the platform cross the line and go to a gate at nearby toilets. Just beyond turn LEFT (disabled person's way out) down the wide tarmaced path.

2 At its bend by a seat follow the waymarked Lôn Gwyrfai ahead to a gate and under the railway, bending right past a railway water tower. A few yards beyond leave the Lôn Gwyrfai and go through a gate on the left into a field. Turn RIGHT and follow a path round the mature tree-lined field edge to a gate and a bridge over a stream to rejoin the

LÔN GWYRFAI

DESCRIPTION A delightful undulating 4½ mile linear walk between Rhyd Ddu and Beddgelert stations, combined with a ride on the Welsh Highland Railway. The route follows Lôn Gwyrfai, a waymarked recreational trail created for walkers, cyclists and horse riders. It features the lovely lake of Llyn-y-Gader, an ancient bridge, the mixed woodland of Beddgelert Forest, close encounters with the railway and great views. The trail can be undertaken in either direction after taking the train from either Beddgelert or Rhyd Ddu, or further along the line. However I have described the route from Rhyd Ddu, as it involves less climbing. You can also use the Sherpa S4 Beddgelert – Caernarfon bus service or enjoy walking the trail both ways. Refreshments are available at The Cwellyn Arms pub and Ty Mawr tea-room in Rhyd Ddu (See end of paragraph 3 in Walk 16 for link path shown). Allow about 3 hours.

START Rhyd Ddu station [SH 571526]

DIRECTIONS Use the SNPA car park below Beddgelert station, signposted from the A498 between the Tourist Information Centre and the Royal Goat Hotel, then take the train to Rhyd Ddu.

Rhyd Ddu was a 19thC slate quarry village, built to provide housing for the men who worked in nearby slate quarries and their families. From 1881 until 1922, when the Welsh Highland Railway was formed, it was the terminus of the North Wales Narrow Gauge Railways and originally called Snowdon. The line carried slate, quarrymen and later tourists attracted by the Rhyd Ddu Path, previously called the Beddgelert Path, up Snowdon. Lying approximately half-way between Caernarfon and Porthmadog Rhyd Ddu station is now a passing and changing point for trains.

From the northern end of the platform cross the railway line by the water tower to a small gate to reach the car park below. From the car park entrance by toilets cross the road with care to an elaborate iron gate

opposite to join the Lôn Gwyrfai. The stony trail heads across reedy terrain towards Mynydd Drws-y-coed, crosses a bridge over the Afon Gwyrfai and passes a bridleway on the right. The gated trail then crosses a narrow fenced causeway – *originally used to transport slate by rail* – past Llyn-y-Gader – to an information board. Go through the nearby gate by an old stone building on the site of the former Gadair-wyllt slate quarry (1885-1920). The trail continues along the Scots pine-covered western side of the lake – *offering a classic view of Snowdon* – then along the edge of Beddgelert Forest, later bending left along a forestry track to a track T-junction.

2 Turn LEFT down the track to a gated crossing of the Welsh Highland Railway near the A4085 at Pont Cae Gors. The trail continues south down a straight wide gravel road past a side track crossing of the railway – *offering great views of any trains* – to the entrance to the Forest car park. The trail continues down the narrower track past Hafod Ruffydd, then turns RIGHT along a side track to cross an 18thC stone bridge over the Afon Cwm Du on the old road to Caernarfon. Follow the narrow track ahead up to recross the railway then continue along the track past the entrance to cottages, rising to an information board at a great viewpoint.

3 Continue ahead down the track, past a side track on the right. Shortly the trail descends a narrow stony path on the right, over a river and through tall pines, then turns left down a stony track. Just before the railway and Beddgelert Forest Campsite turn RIGHT along a forestry track past Meillionen Forest Campsite railway halt. Soon the trail goes up the track's right fork through woodland and past a waymarked path on the left. At a junction bend LEFT down to a footbridge over a stream to a gate beyond out of the forest.

4 The stony trail descends across the open hillside, offering good views, to a gate and continues beside a wall to a gate in it, then descends to a gate by the outbuilding of a house opposite. Turn LEFT down its access

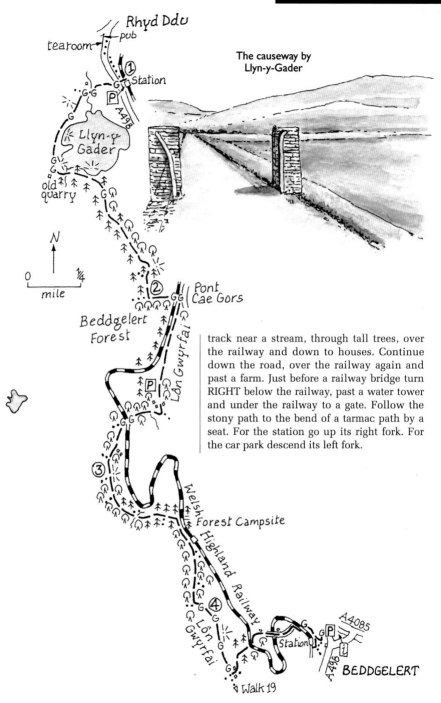

The causeway by
Llyn-y-Gader

track near a stream, through tall trees, over the railway and down to houses. Continue down the road, over the railway again and past a farm. Just before a railway bridge turn RIGHT below the railway, past a water tower and under the railway to a gate. Follow the stony path to the bend of a tarmac path by a seat. For the station go up its right fork. For the car park descend its left fork.

WALK 21
GELERT'S GRAVE

DESCRIPTION A 1¼ mile riverside walk on level paths suitable for wheelchairs and push-chairs, featuring the grave and sculpture of the legendary dog, with which Beddgelert has long been associated. Allow about 1 hour.
START Beddgelert station or SNPA car park below [SH 588482]
DIRECTIONS If arriving by car the car park is signposted from the A498 between the Tourist Information Centre and the Royal Goat Hotel. Follow instructions from paragraph 2.

Gelert
sculpture

*B*eddgelert *is a small picturesque village in the heart of Snowdonia lying at the confluence of the Glaslyn and Colwyn rivers in a valley enclosed by mountains. It is probably named after an 8thC Christian missionary Celert who settled here. Yet it associated with the legend of the hound Gelert, whose 'grave' attracts thousands of visitors each year. It is said to have been created in the late 18thC by the landlord of the Royal Goat Hotel to encourage visitors and it seems to have worked! The village is more recently associated with Alfred Bestall, who wrote and illustrated some of the famous Rupert Bear stories which appeared in the Daily Express last century, whilst he lived in the village, taking inspiration from the beautiful landscape.*

I From the southern end of the platform cross the line and go to a gate at nearby toilets. Either follow the disabled person's path or descend steps and a meandering stony path then turn RIGHT along the tarmaced path bending down a gate into the corner of the car park.

2 From the car park entrance head to the A498. Follow it LEFT past the Tourist Information Centre to the old bridge over the Afon Colwyn. Turn RIGHT along the riverside lane signposted to Gelert's grave/toilets. Just before the footbridge, go through a gate

and follow the wide path south beside the Afon Glaslyn past nearby St Mary's church – *built on the site of a 7thC Augustinian Priory.* Shortly, turn RIGHT to follow another path to Gelert's grave to learn about the legend of the faithful hound and on to a ruin containing a bronze sculpture of the dog.

3 Turn LEFT along another path back to the river. Go through a gate by a small building and continue south alongside the Afon Glaslyn. After crossing a footbridge over the river by the railway bridge, return to Beddgelert along the other side of the river.

WALK 22
ABERGLASLYN PASS (1)

DESCRIPTION A 2¾ mile riverside walk from Beddgelert featuring Gelert's Grave and the stunning Aberglaslyn Pass. The route extends Walk 21 alongside the Afon Glaslyn south for ¾ mile, initially by the railway. Care is needed later on the rocky Fisherman's Path above the river, but you can turn back at any time. Allow about 2 hours.
START As Walk 21.

1-3 Follow instructions in paragraphs 1-3 of Walk 21. After crossing the Afon Glaslyn cross the nearby railway and continue south on a path alongside the river through Aberglaslyn Pass to Pont Aberglaslyn. *Until the early 19thC Aberglaslyn was a small tidal port boasting copper exporting and boat building.* Return along the river to Beddgelert.

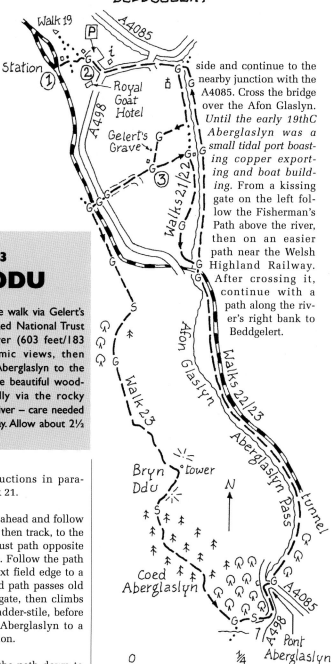

BEDDGELERT

side and continue to the nearby junction with the A4085. Cross the bridge over the Afon Glaslyn. *Until the early 19thC Aberglaslyn was a small tidal port boasting copper exporting and boat building.* From a kissing gate on the left follow the Fisherman's Path above the river, then on an easier path near the Welsh Highland Railway. After crossing it, continue with a path along the river's right bank to Beddgelert.

WALK 23
BRYN DDU

DESCRIPTION A 3¾ mile walk via Gelert's Grave, following a waymarked National Trust path up to Bryn Ddu tower (603 feet/183 metres) offering panoramic views, then descending through Coed Aberglaslyn to the A498. It returns through the beautiful wooded Aberglaslyn Pass, initially via the rocky Fisherman's Path above the river – care needed – then briefly near the railway. Allow about 2½ hours.

START As Walk 21.

1-2 Follow the instructions in paragraphs 1-2 of Walk 21.

3 Go through a small gate ahead and follow the National Trust path, then track, to the A498. Take the National Trust path opposite up to cross the railway line. Follow the path to a gate, then along the next field edge to a ladder-stile. The waymarked path passes old workings, rises to a small gate, then climbs to Bryn Ddu tower and a ladder-stile, before descending through Coed Aberglaslyn to a small gate onto a path junction.

4 Turn LEFT and follow the path down to the A498. Cross with care to the opposite

29

WALK 24
ABERGLASLYN PASS (2)

DESCRIPTION A 2 mile linear walk through the beautiful wooded Aberglaslyn Pass, after a short train ride from Beddgelert station through the Pass and tunnel to Nantmor Halt. One of the area's delights from two different perspectives! From Nantmor the route heads to the National Trust Aberglaslyn car park and passes through woodland to Pont Aberglaslyn. It then follows the river through the Pass, initially via the rocky Fisherman's Path, where care is needed, back to Beddgelert. Allow about 1½ hours. Alternatively you can use the National Trust car, catch a train from Nantmor to Beddgelert and walk back.

START Nantmor Halt [SH599460]

DIRECTIONS Use the SNPA car park below Beddgelert station and catch a Porthmadog bound train to Nantmor – a request stop so please notify the guard before boarding the train.

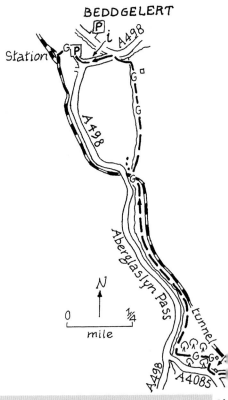

From Nantmor Halt descend the narrow road to the A4085. Follow it RIGHT past a house to the entrance to the National Trust Aberglaslyn car park. Go through a small gate by the ticket machine and toilets and follow the signed path ahead through woodland to Pont Aberglaslyn, then continue north along the Fisherman's Path above the river then on an easier path near the railway. After crossing it continue beside the river to cross a footbridge over it at Beddgelert. Go along the road past toilets to the main road bridge. Cross the road and follow it left to the car park's access road.

WALK 25
NANTMOR VALLEY

DESCRIPTION A delightful scenic 8 mile (**A**) or 6 mile (**B**) walk, featuring magnificent mature woodland and the beautiful Aberglaslyn Pass. After taking the train from Beddgelert through the Aberglaslyn Pass to Nantmor, the route heads across open country into the attractive hidden upland wooded Nanmor valley, associated with the renowned 15thC bard Dafydd Nanmor. It returns by narrow undulating scenic roads to Nantmor, then follows the river back through the Aberglaslyn Pass to Beddgelert. Allow about 4½ and 3½ hours respectively. Alternatively, the route can be undertaken as a 6 mile (**A**) or 4 mile (**B**) circular walk to and from Nantmor Halt by train or slightly longer from the National Trust Aberglaslyn car park.

Allow about 3½ and 2½ hours.
START Nantmor Halt [SH599460]
DIRECTIONS Use the SNPA car park below Beddgelert station and catch a train to Nantmor Halt or from further along the line if doing just the circular walks. Nantmor is a request stop so notify the guard prior to boarding the train.

From Nantmor Halt go up the road then at a chapel turn LEFT up a side road to a gate by stables and Cilfynydd. Follow the signposted path past a small rock outcrop and the smaller of two telegraph poles, then over streams. Go along the left-hand reedy field edge by a fence, then RIGHT along a wall to a kissing gate. Follow a path near the stream to a signed wall gap. Pass to the right of trees ahead, then go slightly left up the field to a gap in the wall onto a minor road above by a cottage. Turn LEFT up the road to its end at a farm.

2 Go through a waymarked gate and another opposite. Descend the field edge below the house to a kissing gate. Continue down the field to a gate. Keep ahead, then at a telegraph pole angle RIGHT to an old wall. Turn RIGHT down a wide stony path beside it. Follow the path across a reedy area, then LEFT along its edge, through a wall gap and on more or less parallel with the wall. Just before the wide path begins to descend follow a faint path down to join the wall and on to a gate. Cross a stream and follow the path to a stone stile and along the edge of woodland to where it splits. (For **Walk B** descend the wide right fork to a ladder-stile/gate and barn beyond. Angle left across the field to a ladder-stile, cross a footbridge over a river, and continue up to the valley road at point 4).

3 For **Walk A** follow the path ahead up through the wood – *full of bluebells in Spring* – and through a wall gap. The path meanders up then soon descends and continues to a stream. Take the waymarked left fork to pass behind a nearby cottage. After passing a small ruin descend the path's waymarked right fork through woodland to a ladder-stile/gate, then out of trees to pass through two small gates – *with a good view into the wooded Nanmor valley*. The path passes in front of a cottage, crosses its access track, then goes to a ladder-stile ahead. It continues through woodland by the river Nanmor to a gate then a ladder-stile onto a minor road by a bridge over the river. Follow the quiet narrow scenic road south along the wooded upland Nanmor valley, later descending in stages and passing a house to be joined by Walk B.

4 Follow the undulating road along the valley, later descending to pass the substantial early 19thC house of Cae Dafydd, linked by name to the 15thC bard Dafydd Nanmor. At a junction by a cottage turn RIGHT along a narrow side road, over river and through mature woodland. The undulating road later descends in stages – *with a good view of Moel Hebog* – to Nantmor. Now follow instructions in Walk 24 for the return to Beddgelert through the Aberglaslyn Pass.

WALK 26

CWM BYCHAN & LLYN DINAS

DESCRIPTION A 5¾ mile circular walk from Beddgelert of great variety. After a leisurely walk along the beautiful Aberglaslyn Pass, the route climbs steadily up the hidden upland valley of Cwm Bychan mined for copper from the late 18thC until 1930 and containing the remains of an aerial ropeway. After reaching a height of 951 ft/290 metres it descends to the end of beautiful Llyn Dinas, then returns past Sygun Copper Mine, with Visitor Centre and café. Allow about 4 hours.

An alternative 4¼ mile linear walk is to take a short train ride from Beddgelert through Aberglaslyn Pass to Nantmor Halt – a request stop so notify the guard prior to boarding the train – then follow this route back. Allow about 3 hours. After alighting at Nantmor Halt descend the narrow road to the A4085. Follow it right to the National Trust Aberglaslyn car park. Go through a small gate by the ticket machine and toilets and follow instructions in paragraph 2.
START Beddgelert station or SNPA car park below [SH 588482].
Nantmor Halt [SH599460] for the linear walk.

I From the southern end of the platform at Beddgelert station cross the line and go to a gate at nearby toilets. Follow a path down to the car park. From its entrance head to the A498. Follow it LEFT past the Tourist Information Centre to the old bridge over the Afon Colwyn. Turn RIGHT along the riverside lane signposted to Gelert's grave/toilets and cross the footbridge over the Afon Glaslyn. Now follow a path south beside the river, later crossing the railway, then continuing beside it before it enters a tunnel. After the rocky Fisherman's Path above the river – *care needed* – you reach Pont Aberglaslyn. Here turn LEFT and follow a path through woodland to a path junction just before a gate at toilets in the National Trust car park. Turn LEFT.

2 Follow the path signposted to Cwm Bychan under the railway bridge, up through woodland and on to a small gate. The path briefly accompanies the stream, then rises steadily up Cwm Bychan, later passing pylons – *the former aerial ropeway built in 1928 to carry ore down the valley from a copper mine. It was then taken by horse and cart to Porthmadog and shipped to South Wales for making into copper.* The path rises steadily past a ruin and waste tip on your right, later becoming more enclosed by heather/boulder covered ridges. Cross a ladder-stile at the highest point – *with views of Snowdon, Moel Siabod, and Cnicht.* Follow the path LEFT to a finger post at the top of Grib Ddu.

3 Turn RIGHT down the stony path signposted to Llyn Dinas. The path begins a long steady descent, later levelling out, before a final steeper descent to the end of the lake. Go through a nearby kissing gate and past the large footbridge over the Afon Glaslyn. Follow a path, initially near the river, to a road leading to Sygun Copper Mine. Go up the road and just beyond the car park entrance, turn RIGHT along a way-marked path beside a wall, past a house to join a minor road.

4 Follow the road for about ½ mile. Just before it crosses the river to the A498 go through a kissing gate and follow the riverside path to cross the footbridge over the river into Beddgelert.

WALK 27

CWM BYCHAN & SYGUN

DESCRIPTION This route offers a shorter variation of Walk 26 – a circular 5 mile walk from Beddgelert and a 3½ mile linear walk from Nantmor Halt after a short train ride. After climbing up Cwm Bychan it descends via Bwlch-y-Sygyn directly to 19thC Sygun underground copper mine, with its Visitor Centre and café. Mining began at Sygun in the early 19thC until

its closure in 1903. Since 1986 the mine has been open to the public. Allow about 3½ and 2½ hours.
START As Walk 26.

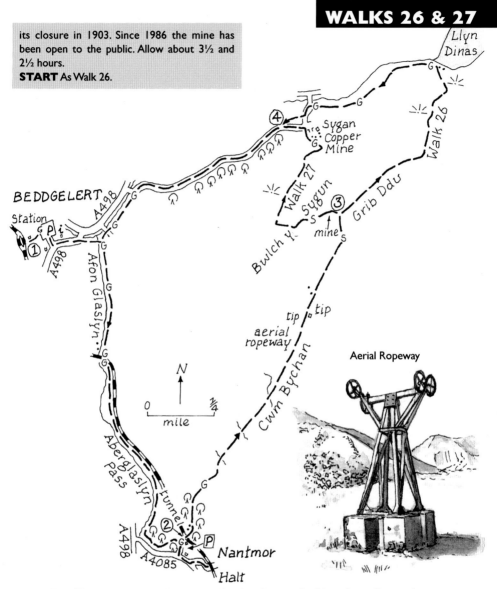

Aerial Ropeway

1-2
Follow instructions in paragraphs 1-2 of Walk 26.

3
Turn LEFT signposted to Beddgelert/ Sygun, passing through an old mine to cross a ladder-stile. Turn LEFT up a path by the fence, then RIGHT at its corner to follow an initially stony path down to a junction of paths by a large boulder in a flat area at Bwlch-y-Sygyn. Turn RIGHT to a good view-

point overlooking the valley and across to Snowdon. The stony path now descends past a path on the left and continues down the steep rhododendron-covered hillside. Later it passes the entrance to Sygun mine, then a path leading to the Visitor Centre to reach a minor road. Turn LEFT along it.

4
Follow instructions in paragraph 4 of Walk 26.

WALK 28

PONT CROESOR

DESCRIPTION A 2¾ mile linear walk from Pont Croesor across the low-lying reclaimed land of Traeth Mawr to Porthmadog, after a short ride on the railway. The route features close encounters with both the Welsh Highland Railway and Welsh Highland Heritage Railway and joins part of a waymarked Circular Route into Porthmadog. First there is an opportunity to visit the Glaslyn Osprey Viewing Centre at Pont Croesor to see live close-up pictures of this breeding spectacular fish-eating bird of prey, sadly an endangered species. Allow about 2 hours.

START Pont Croesor [SH 593413]

DIRECTIONS Use the large long stay Llyn Bach car park just past the Wilco store as shown. At its corner by Wilco's car park is a kissing-gated crossing of the Welsh Highland Railway. Follow the surfaced path beside the railway to Pont Britannia by the harbour and station. Catch a train from Porthmadog station to Pont Croesor – a request stop so please notify the guard before boarding the train.

*I*n 2004 a pair of ospreys were discovered breeding in the Glaslyn area – the first official recording in Wales. As a result the Glaslyn Osprey Project was established, led by the RSPB, to offer 24 hours a day monitoring protection and a viewing site for the public. Several successful breeding years followed for the ospreys who returned every year from Africa in early Spring to the same nesting site. In 2113 the running of the Project was handed over to Bywyd Gwyllt Galslyn Wildlife, a local community interest not for profit company, whose work is mainly undertaken by volunteers. 2015 saw the opening of a Visitor Information Centre by Welsh naturalist and TV presenter Iolo Williams and the start of live website streaming. There are now two pairs of breeding ospreys.

I Go along the platform past toilets, then follow the signed pedestrian route to the nearby Osprey Viewing Centre, where light refreshments are available. Return and pass through the large car park to its entrance. Follow the B4410 with care facing oncoming traffic to the A498 at Prenteg. Continue along the grass verge then take a stony track angling left past houses and a former chapel to a small gate on its bend. Follow the part paved path along the large field edge above a stream to a small stone barn and on to a gate. The kissing gated path goes along the edge of two fields to a stony track. Follow it up to where it crosses a bridge over the Welsh Highland Railway.

2 Here go through a small gate and descend to the railway. Follow the gated path by the railway along the edge of two fields, across the railway and up to a bridge over it. A narrow gated path enclosed by a wall and fence continues below the railway to a crossing bridleway by Cynfal and on to another signed bridleway/road. Here you join the waymarked Circular Route (CR) for the journey into Porthmadog. Follow the CR ahead beside the railway past Pen-y-Mount Junction – *the northern terminus of the Welsh Highland Heritage Railway (WHHR), which opened in 1980. See Walk 29 for more information.* Soon the path crosses the WHR and continues between the two sets of narrow gauge railways.

3 After passing under the by-pass, the CR path leaves the WHR and passes the WHHR's engine sheds to a gated crossing of the mainline railway, then follows a road through a small industrial estate. After crossing a bridge over a water-filled drain, the CR turns LEFT along a road to a T-junction by the incoming WHR. Follow a short fenced path opposite by the railway, then cross it and take a path into and along the edge of a small park adjoining Llyn Bach – *created as a flood control pool for the harbour when it was built* – soon by the railway, to a gated crossing to the car park, or continue along the surfaced path beside the railway to Pont Britannia by the harbour and station.

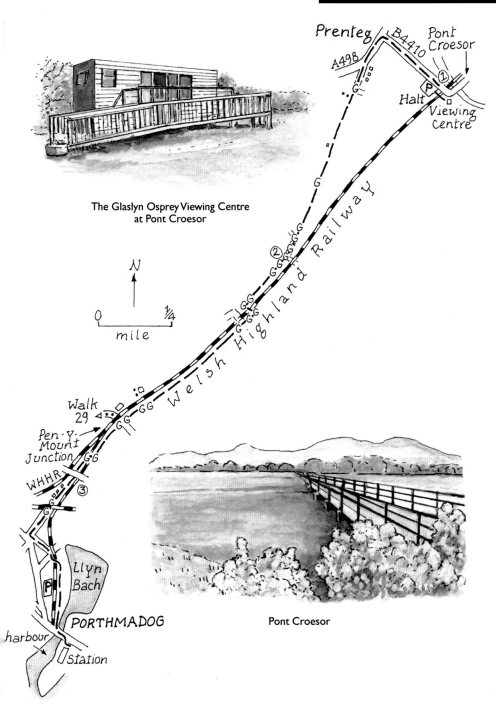

The Glaslyn Osprey Viewing Centre
at Pont Croesor

Prenteg

B4410

Pont Croesor

A498

Halt

Viewing Centre

N

0   ¼
mile

Welsh Highland Railway

Walk 29

Pen-y-Mount Junction

WHHR

Llyn Bach

PORTHMADOG

harbour

Station

Pont Croesor

35

TREMADOG

DESCRIPTION A 3½ mile walk following part of a waymarked Circular Route linking Porthmadog and Tremadog. The route takes you from the harbour, passes close to the Welsh Highland Railway (WHR) and adjoining Welsh Highland Heritage Railway (WHHR), then continues to the attractive historic Nursery Wood and the attractive planned early 19thC settlement of Tremadog, with its award-winning fish & chip shop. It then follows the route of a former tramway and canal back to Porthmadog to the WHHR station and tea-room, with the opportunity for a short rail journey on its short reconstructed line and a visit to its engine sheds. Allow about 2 hours.

START Porthmadog station [SH 571384]

DIRECTIONS If arriving by car use the large long stay Llyn Bach car park just past the Wilco store as shown. At its corner by Wilco's car park is a kissing-gated crossing of the railway where you can join the route

Tremadog, just north of Porthmadog, was founded by William Maddocks on former estuary land drained as part of his ambitious land reclamation project, which included the building of The Cob across Traeth Mawr (See Walk). It is a fine example of a planned town, whose centre, with its distinctive square, largely unaltered today, completed by 1811. It contains a Gothic revival style church and an iconic classical Greek Temple style fronted chapel. The main streets were named Dublin Street and London Street by Maddocks in anticipation of Tremadog becoming a staging post on a proposed major route from London to Ireland via a new port at Porth Dinllaen on the Llyn Peninsula. Unfortunately Holyhead was chosen as the ferry port instead. Maddocks also built a water-powered mill for carding and spinning nearby to develop the local woollen industry. T E Lawrence, better known as Lawrence of Arabia, was born here in 1888.

Nursery Wood was originally established by Maddocks as a tree nursery to sup-

ply timber to local ship building yards. It continued as a nursery into the early 20thC but is now attractive mature community woodland.

The Welsh Highland Heritage Railway is a short reconstructed narrow gauge railway that predates and is separate from the more recently restored Welsh Highland Railway. It is operated by a member owned charity and run primarily by volunteers. It uses two vintage steam locomotives and restored carriages to run trains 1 mile to Pen-y-Mount station. It also has a museum, displays & tearoom.

I After alighting from the train follow the line back past Spooner's and the pavement across Pont Brittania by the harbour. Cross the road and follow a tarmaced path beside the railway above the river to a kissing-gated crossing by the car park. Follow a path along the edge of the small park adjoining Llyn Bach, soon angling left to cross the railway. Follow an enclosed path beside it to a road. Go along the one-way road opposite on a signposted Circular Route (CR) past the garage. At a junction turn with the CR across the bridge over the water-filled drain, known as Y Cyt, and along the road through a small industrial estate, then over the gated mainline railway crossing. The CR goes past engine sheds by the narrow gauge sidings of the Welsh Highland Heritage Railway (WHHR), then angles right and continues enclosed between the WHR and the WHHR with its various rolling stock, passing under the bypass. After a gated crossing the path continues on the other side of the WHR past Pen-y-Mount station – *the northern terminus of the WHHR, which opened in 1980* – to a gate onto a road.

2 Here the CR crosses the railway line and continues along the straight quiet road past dwellings to a roundabout at the by-pass. Turn RIGHT along the pavement. Soon the CR goes through a gate into Nursery Wood. Ignore a footbridge on the left and a path on the right, but follow the main path beside the stream through the attractive mature woodland to a T-junction at the

tion. Follow your outward road ahead to the T-junction by the WHR.

4 Turn LEFT along the right-hand edge of the road, then follow a wide surfaced walkway with seats between Llyn Bach and the water of Traeth Mawr to tidal gates, which regulate the tidal flow of the Afon Glaslyn Just beyond bear RIGHT to follow a path along the edge of Ynys Tywyn, a small wooded knoll

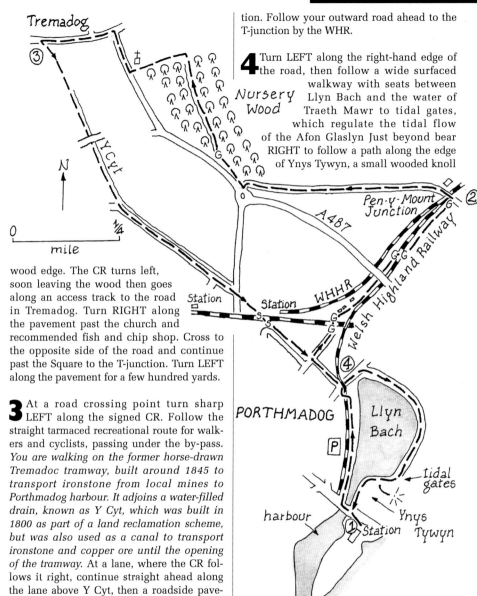

wood edge. The CR turns left, soon leaving the wood then goes along an access track to the road in Tremadog. Turn RIGHT along the pavement past the church and recommended fish and chip shop. Cross to the opposite side of the road and continue past the Square to the T-junction. Turn LEFT along the pavement for a few hundred yards.

3 At a road crossing point turn sharp LEFT along the signed CR. Follow the straight tarmaced recreational route for walkers and cyclists, passing under the by-pass. *You are walking on the former horse-drawn Tremadoc tramway, built around 1845 to transport ironstone from local mines to Porthmadog harbour. It adjoins a water-filled drain, known as Y Cyt, which was built in 1800 as part of a land reclamation scheme, but was also used as a canal to transport ironstone and copper ore until the opening of the tramway.* At a lane, where the CR follows it right, continue straight ahead along the lane above Y Cyt, then a roadside pavement to the main road in Porthmadog by the Queens Hotel. Cross the road and turn RIGHT along the pavement, then LEFT along the edge of the WHHR car park to its station entrance and a stiled crossing of the main-line railway onto the bend of a road. Follow a raised grass path by the road overlooking the water-filled drain to a familiar road junc-

owned by the National Trust. Soon take a stepped path up to a good viewpoint, then return to continue with the main path to emerge onto the main road opposite the station complex.

BORTH-Y-GEST

DESCRIPTION A 3¾ mile walk following the Wales Coast Path from Porthmadog to the small picturesque coastal village of Borth-y-Gest, with its small sandy bay, Victorian houses, cafe and delightful estuary views. The walk returns across a wooded shoulder beneath the eastern end of Moel-y-Gest down to Porthmadog. It then follows an interesting route through the town, passing the Welsh Highland Heritage Railway station (See Walk 29 for information) and accompanying the Welsh Highland Railway to the start. Allow about 2½ hours.
START Porthmadog station [SH 571384]
DIRECTIONS If arriving by car use the large long stay Llyn Bach car park just past the Wilco store as shown. At its corner by Wilco's car park is a kissing-gated.

The building of The Cob (See Walk 32) led to the creation of Porthmadog as a flourishing town and seaport. The diverted river created a natural harbour, deep enough for ocean going sailing ships. A new port opened in 1825 and became known as Port Madoc. From the beginning it served the slate quarries of the Ffestiniog area, with slate initially carried in small boats down the Dwyryd and transferred onto sea-going vessels. In 1836 the opening of the Ffestiniog Railway enabled slate to be transported directly from the quarries to the port. From here slate was exported all over the world and a town began to rapidly grow alongside it. At its peak over 1000 vessels used the harbour in any one year. There was also a thriving ship building industry and its three-masted schooners, built up to 1913 to carry slate, were the last wooden merchant ships to be built in the UK. It was also a busy port for salted cod.

Following the arrival of the Cambrian Railway in 1867, which offered an alternative means of transporting slate to Britain's developing industrial towns, trade began to decline, and the loss of the German slate market at the start of World War I led to the port's final demise. By 1945 the last of the

slate ships had gone and a year later the Ffestiniog Railway closed. Today Porthmadog, as it was renamed in 1974, is an attractive historic tourist destination, with the town now uniquely the terminus of two restored historic steam-operated narrow gauge railways, and an important sailing centre.

Borth-y-Gest, one mile south of Porthmadog, with its small sheltered bay, was once the start of a key route for travellers, guided by locals, across the wide treacherous Glaslyn estuary to Harlech. Ships were built here until the development of Porthmadog.

After alighting from the train follow the line back past Spooner's and the pavement across Pont Brittania over the river. Now follow the signposted Wales Coast Path (WCP) above the harbour, past the Harbourmaster's office and nearby Maritime Museum to an information board. Continue round the harbour past the slipway to join the road beneath the large former sea captain's houses. Follow this quiet access road past small boatyards and other maritime businesses to its end at Madog Boatyard. Here the WCP rises and passes between houses to join a road. Descend it then steps to the shore at Borth-y-Gest. Walk along the pavement past the small bay (or along the beach if tidal conditions permit to steps at the other side) past Seaview Café Bistro and Coffee Lounge opposite then along the edge of a car park, with toilets and information boards. At the far end the signposted WCP joins the adjoining road. When it bends right go along another road ahead above the shoreline – *offering panoramic views along the estuary* – round to its end at the village church and an information board on Pen y Banc Nature Reserve. Retrace your steps.

2 At the northern end of the bay take a signposted path on the left past Borth Wen along a stony track, then between a field and woodland up to a gate and on along a field edge to a kissing gate. Follow the wide path through open woodland to a small gate by a house. Go up its access road and down to a junction. Turn RIGHT along the road to

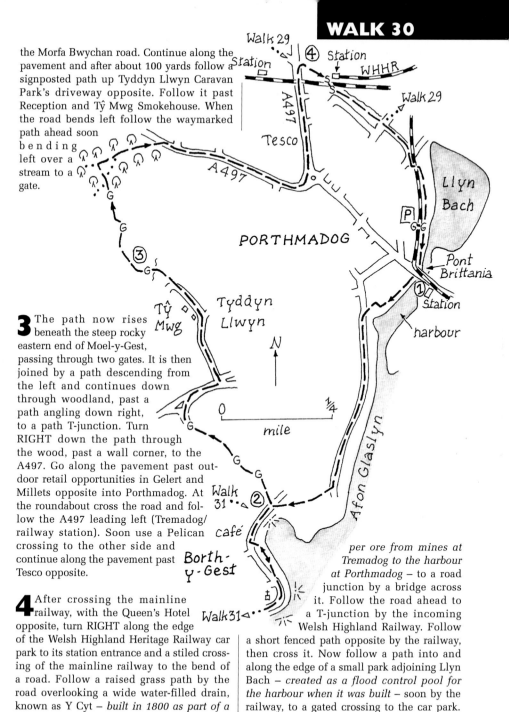

the Morfa Bwychan road. Continue along the pavement and after about 100 yards follow a signposted path up Tyddyn Llwyn Caravan Park's driveway opposite. Follow it past Reception and Tŷ Mwg Smokehouse. When the road bends left follow the waymarked path ahead soon bending left over a stream to a gate.

3 The path now rises beneath the steep rocky eastern end of Moel-y-Gest, passing through two gates. It is then joined by a path descending from the left and continues down through woodland, past a path angling down right, to a path T-junction. Turn RIGHT down the path through the wood, past a wall corner, to the A497. Go along the pavement past outdoor retail opportunities in Gelert and Millets opposite into Porthmadog. At the roundabout cross the road and follow the A497 leading left (Tremadog/railway station). Soon use a Pelican crossing to the other side and continue along the pavement past Tesco opposite.

4 After crossing the mainline railway, with the Queen's Hotel opposite, turn RIGHT along the edge of the Welsh Highland Heritage Railway car park to its station entrance and a stiled crossing of the mainline railway to the bend of a road. Follow a raised grass path by the road overlooking a wide water-filled drain, known as Y Cyt – *built in 1800 as part of a land reclamation scheme, but used for a time as a canal to transport ironstone and cop-* per ore from mines at Tremadog to the harbour at Porthmadog – to a road junction by a bridge across it. Follow the road ahead to a T-junction by the incoming Welsh Highland Railway. Follow a short fenced path opposite by the railway, then cross it. Now follow a path into and along the edge of a small park adjoining Llyn Bach – *created as a flood control pool for the harbour when it was built* – soon by the railway, to a gated crossing to the car park. Follow the surfaced path beside the railway, then cross Pont Britannia to the station.

MORFA BWYCHAN

DESCRIPTION A 5¼ mile walk **(A)** featuring a fine section of coastline offering lovely views, a stroll along popular Black Rock Sands, and two Nature Reserves. A 4 mile walk **(B)** omitting Black Rock Sands is included. The route follows the Wales Coast Path to the picturesque village of Borth-y-Gest, passes through Pen y Banc Nature Reserve and continues to Morfa Bwychan (Black Rock Sands). Walk B heads inland but Walk A follows the Wales Coast Path to the small headland of Ynys Cyngar then along the edge of the beach overlooked by dunes. It then turns inland to the holiday village before crossing the golf club to join Walk B. After a section of pavement walking, the route then returns through the delightful mature woodland of Parc y Borth Nature Reserve to Borth-y-Gest to follow the Wales Coast Path back to Porthmadog. Allow about 3 & 2 hours respectively.

START Porthmadog station [SH 571384]

DIRECTIONS If arriving by car use the large long stay Llyn Bach car park just past the Wilco store as shown. At its corner by Wilco's car park is a kissing-gated crossing of the railway. Follow a surfaced path beside the railway to join the route at Pont Britannia by the harbour.

I After alighting from the train follow the line back past Spooner's, then the pavement across Pont Brittania over the river. Now follow the signposted Wales Coast Path (WCP) above the harbour, past the Harbourmaster's office and nearby Maritime Museum to an information board. Continue round the harbour past the slipway to join the road beneath the large former sea captain's houses. Follow this quiet access road past small boatyards and other maritime businesses to its end at Madog Boatyard. Here the WCP rises and passes between houses to join a road. Descend it then steps to the shore at Borth-y-Gest. Walk along the pavement past the small bay (or along the beach if tidal conditions permit

to steps at the other side) past Seaview Café Bistro and Coffee Lounge opposite, then along the edge of a car park with toilets and information boards. At the far end the signposted WCP joins the adjoining road. When it bends right go along another road ahead above the shoreline – *offering extensive panoramic views along the estuary* – round to its end at the village church and an information board on Pen y Banc Nature Reserve – *consisting of secluded coves, coastal rocks, sand dunes, mixed woodland, scrub & heath.*

2 Follow the WCP through the Reserve past stepped paths to the beach. At a boardwalked path junction the WCP turns right past a path leading to a viewpoint, rising through trees to a narrow stony access track. The WCP follows it left past dwellings, then a path through trees and scrub, past side paths, and over a lane. Shortly, at a path junction it descends then continues to a finger post at a path junction just above the beach at Morfa Bychan. (For **Walk B** follow the path inland, soon fenced, along the

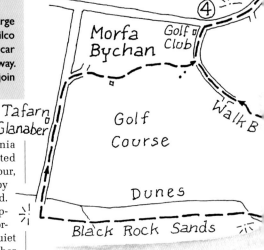

perimeter of the golf course to join the access road from nearby Glasfryn. It passes other properties then joins a road leading from the golf course. Follow it to a road junction by the golf club at point 4).

3 The WCP enters National Trust owned Morfa Bychan and follows the perimeter of the golf course just above the delightful sandy beach around the bay and past a house on Ynys Cyngar, then down to the beach – *with a good view across the estuary to Harlech, its castle and the Rhinog mountains beyond.* Continue along the beach – *an extensive area of sand at low tide overlooked by dunes and the only UK beach to allow vehicles onto it* – shortly crossing a stream flowing onto it. With a view ahead of Criccieth Castle, at a finger post signposting toilets, turn RIGHT to join a road passing through the dunes and

the toilets. Follow a pink roadside walkway past several holiday parks and the Tafarn Glanaber pub. At the first dwellings of Morfa Bychan village turn RIGHT along a road. Just after it bends left turn RIGHT along a signposted path, over a stream and on through trees to the golf course. Follow the waymarked narrow stony track, shortly joined by another, to a road. Follow it to a T-junction by the golf club.

4 Turn right along the wide roadside pavement – *with a view of craggy Moel y Gest* – rising past Penllyn to the entrance to Blackrock Llama Centre and new mountain views. The road now descends past Moelfre. Just before the next house take a signposted path angling up to a gate just beyond an information board into Parc y Borth Nature Reserve. Follow the path to a path junction at a white-topped post and turn RIGHT. Follow the path through delightful mature oak woodland, full of bluebells in Spring, to a small gate and down to another. Descend the enclosed path between houses, then steps and follow a stony track to the seafront in Borth-y-Gest. Here you have another opportunity to enjoy refreshments before returning along your outward route.

WALK 32
THE COB

DESCRIPTION A 4 mile **(A)** or 2¾ mile **(B)** walk from the terminus of both the Welsh Highland and Ffestiniog Railways, full of interest and with great views, The route follows the Ffestiniog Railway across The Cob to Traeth Glaslyn Nature Reserve, offering perhaps a close encounter with a Ffestiniog Railway steam train. Walk A continues with the Wales Coast Path for a short circuit on a small headland, for new views, then returns with Walk B along a surfaced cycle/walkway on the eastern side of The Cob. It then visits Ynys Tywyn, a small rocky knoll and crosses the tidal gates for a delightful walk around Llyn Bach. Allow about 2½ hours.

START Porthmadog station [SH 572384]

DIRECTIONS If arriving by car use the large long stay Llyn Bach car park just past the Wilco store as shown. At its corner by Wilco's car park is a kissing-gated crossing of the railway. Follow the surfaced path beside the railway to the main road and go across Pont Brittania. The enclosed path across The Cob starts from the roadside by Spooner's, part of the station complex.

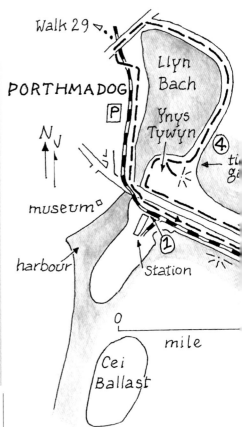

*F**or centuries** crossing the wide upper Glasfryn estuary, known as Traeth Mawr, was dangerous because of the strong tides or soft sands. It was left to William Maddocks (1774-1828) to have the necessary vision, commitment and financial resources to tame it. His ambitious proposal, which received Parliamentary consent, was for a stone embankment across the mouth of the estuary to keep out the sea. Hundreds of men were involved in the mammoth task, starting from both ends, and an old ship full of rocks was sunk to bridge the gap between them. Finally, after several years of endeavour and at a cost of £160,000 – a considerable amount of money in those days – on 11th September 1811 the one mile long embankment, known as The Cob, with a toll road, was opened, with due celebration. Unfortunately early the following year the embankment was breached by the sea. After necessary repair work it reopened in 1814 and it has stood the test of time for over two hundred hundred years,*

surviving further severe storm damage on occasions. The building of the embankment caused the diversion of the channel of the Afon Glaslyn and altered forever the nature of the hitherto large upper estuary, Treath Mawr, large parts of which were reclaimed for agricultural land. The Ffestiniog Railway opened in 1836 as a horse and gravity single narrow-gauge tramway linking slate quarries at Blaenau Ffestiniog with the new Port Madoc, where slate was loaded onto sea-going vessels. In 1863 small purpose built steam locomotives were introduced and a year later the railway was allowed to carry passengers. In subsequent decades slate traffic gradually declined but by the 1920s summer tourism traffic had become increasingly important. The Second World War brought an end to both slate and passenger traffic and the line closed in 1946. However after years of mainly voluntary effort and the overcoming of numerous obstacles, in 1983 the 13½ mile railway reopened and now carries thousands of visitors each year.

I At the southern end of the platform, where you alight, cross the line to a stony path overlooking the road. Follow the path across The Cob beside the Ffestiniog Railway. At its end descend steps and cross to the pavement opposite. Nearby are Boston Works and engine sheds – *the main workshops of the Ffestiniog Railway since 1847. Originally the site provided workshops, stables and barracks during the building of The Cob and also stone from a quarry for the embankment itself.* Turn RIGHT to join the

Traeth Mawr

Ffestiniog Railway
The Cob

hide

Boston Works

adjoining wide surfaced Wales Coast Path/NCR 8 and follow it past a building. Just beyond information boards and a bench go a kissing gate on the left gives access to a nearby bird hide in Traeth Glaslyn Nature Reserve. (For **Walk B** continue from paragraph 3.)

2 For **Walk A** go through the cycle arch and past a small layby and at its end cross to a finger post opposite. Follow the Wales Coast Path (WCP) up to cross a road then the Ffestiniog Railway to a small gate. Go up the waymarked WCP then when it continues ahead (your return route), turn LEFT up a side path along the edge of a small wood onto the bend of a stony track. Follow it ahead, rising steadily to a gate and down to a signposted crossroad of bridleways/stony tracks, where you rejoin the WCP. Follow it RIGHT along the track to

a gate by farm buildings at a great viewpoint. When the track bends left to a gate turn RIGHT past a nearby small gate and along the field edge. Follow the path across the field bending left to a WCP waymarked gate. The delightful path makes a long steady descent through woodland via a gate to join your outward route. Return to point 2.

3 Follow the WCP/cycle/walkway below the road across the former estuary, enjoying increasing views east. At its end go along the pavement, past the railway station opposite and Cob Records then turn RIGHT signposted to Ynys Tywyn. Go past a rising stepped path and over a slate stile, then follow the path above the river beneath the tree covered knoll of Ynys Tywyn. Shortly go up a stepped path on the right to a great viewpoint on the south side of Ynys Tywyn, then return to the main path to enter an open area. Bear LEFT to join an enclosed path passing the Environment Agency's controlled tidal gates, which regulate the tidal flow of the Afon Glaslyn.

4 Go along the wide surfaced walkway between Llyn Bach *– created as a flood control pool for the harbour when it was built –* and Traeth Mawr. At its end bear LEFT along a road. After crossing the Welsh Highland Railway turn LEFT along a signposted fenced path then cross the railway line. Now follow a path into and along the edge of a small park, soon by the railway, to the gated crossing to the car park. Follow the surfaced path beside the railway, then cross Pont Britannia to the station.

KEY TO THE MAPS

- ➡   Walk route and direction
- ———   Metalled road
- ---   Unsurfaced road
- ••••   Footpath/route adjoining walk route
- ∿∿➔   River/stream
- ♣ ♤   Trees
- ▪️▪️   Railway
- **G**   Gate
- **S**   Stile
- F.B.   Footbridge
- ⩊   Viewpoint
- P   Parking
- T   Telephone

THE COUNTRYSIDE CODE

- Be safe – plan ahead and follow any signs
- Leave gates and property as you find them
- Protect plants and animals, and take your litter home
- Keep dogs under close control
- Consider other people

Open Access
Some routes cross areas of land where walkers have the legal right of access under The CRoW Act 2000 introduced in May 2005. Access can be subject to restrictions and closure for land management or safety reasons for up to 28 days a year. Details from: www.naturalresourceswales.gov.uk. Please respect any notices.

Pont Croesor, Nantmor, Snowdon Ranger, Tryfan Junction, Dinas and Bontnewydd are request stops so please notify the guard prior to boarding the train. Intending passengers should give a clear signal to the engine driver as the train approaches.

Useful contacts

Welsh Highland Railway 01766 516024
www.festrail.co.uk
Gwynedd Council Rights of Way
www.gwynedd.gov.uk

About the author David Berry

David is an experienced walker with a love of the countryside and an interest in local history. He is the author of a series of walks guidebooks covering North Wales, where he has lived and worked for many years. He has written for Walking Wales and Ramblers Walk magazine, worked as a Rights of Way surveyor across North Wales and served as a member of Denbighshire Local Access Forum. Whether on a riverside ramble, mountain or long distance walk, he greatly appreciates the beauty, culture and history of the landscape and hopes that his comprehensive guidebooks will encourage people to explore on foot its diverse scenery and rich heritage. For more information visit: www.davidberrywalks.co.uk

---

Published by **Kittiwake Books Limited**
3 Glantwymyn Village Workshops, Glantwymyn, Machynlleth, Montgomeryshire SY20 8LY

© Text & map research: David Berry 2018
© Maps & illustrations: Kittiwake-Books Ltd 2018
Drawings by Morag Perrott
Cover photos: Main: Train in Aberglaslyn Pass.
Inset: Passing train (Walk 20). David Berry.

Care has been taken to be accurate. However neither the author nor the publisher can accept responsibility for any errors which may appear, or their consequences. If you are in any doubt about access, check before you proceed.

Printed by Mixam UK.

ISBN: **978 1 908748 53 9**